INTRO

Since it was first seen in 2009, a certain small, independent video game has become something of a phenomenon. We're talking, of course, about Minecraft, the maddenly addictive mix of creativity, building, combat, crafting and survival.

This book will take you through the very early stages of Minecraft (with simple tips to help you get up and running for the first time), then gradually explore in more depth the strategies and approaches you can deploy to get even more out of the game. By the time you get to the end, we've got a whole host of more advanced things that you can try too.

The possibilities of Minecraft are near endless, and we hope that what you're about to read really helps you get as much as possible out of what is a quite brilliant computer game.

Just turn the page to begin your adventure. If all goes to plan, pretty soon you'll be a Minecraft player to be reckoned with!

Published by Dennis Publishing Ltd. 30 Cleveland St, London. W1T 4JD. Company registered in England. **www.dennis.co.uk**

Editorial: Aaron Birch, James Hunt, Simon Brew
Art Editor: Laura Passmore
Production Editor: Rachel Storry
Production: Stephen Catherall

Publisher Dharmesh Mistry
Group MD Ian Westwood
Operations Director Robin Ryan
MD of Advertising Julian Lloyd-Evans
Newstrade Director David Barker
Chief Operating Officer Brett Reynolds
Group Finance Director Ian Leggett
Chief Executive James Tye
Company Founder Felix Dennis

PRINT Polestar
DISTRIBUTION Seymour Distribution

LICENSING & SYNDICATION
To license this product please contact **Carlotta Serantoni** on +44 (0) 20 79076550 or email carlotta_serantoni@dennis.co.uk
To syndicate content from this product please contact **Ryan Chambers** on +44(0) 20 7907 6132 or email Ryan_Chambers@dennis.co.uk

DISCLAIMER

LIABILITY
While every care was taken during the production of this MagBook, the publishers cannot be held responsible for any errors or omissions in it. The paper used within this MagBook is produced from sustainable fibre and are manufactured by mills with a valid chain of custody.

CONTENTS

8-11	ORIGINS OF MINECRAFT
12-13	FORMATS
14-17	BASICS & GAME MODES
18-19	10 TIPS
22-25	CRAFTING ESSENTIALS
26-31	MOBS
34-37	NEVER DIG UP
38-41	STAYING ALIVE
42-47	FURNISHING YOUR HOME
48-51	DEFENDING YOUR HOME
52-57	FARMING
58-59	ANIMAL TAMING
60-63	COOKBOOK
64-65	BIOMES GUIDE
66-67	MINECARTS
68-71	NPC VILLAGES
72-75	VILLAGER TRADING

p34

p58

p72

76-77	**SWORDPLAY**
78-79	**GONE FISHIN'**
80-81	**TEMPLES**
84-87	**CIRCUITS**
88-91	**NETHER PORTALS**
92-95	**THE NETHER**
96-99	**ENCHANTMENTS**
100-103	**POTION BREWING**
104-105	**BEACONS**
106-109	**WINNING MINECRAFT: THE END**
110-111	**WINNING MINECRAFT: THE WITHER**
114-117	**SECRET BLOCKS AND ITEMS**
118-121	**TECHNICAL SECRETS**
122-125	**SETTINGS AND TWEAKS**
126-129	**PLAYING MINECRAFT ONLINE**
132-135	**MODS, SKINS & UPDATES**
136-139	**BLOCK ID LIST**
140-147	**CRAFTING GLOSSARY**

p78

p96

p104

MINECRAFT:

Finding your way into the world of Minecraft fortunately isn't the most difficult job. But that doesn't mean it's always the kind of game you can jump straight into and hope to get the best out of. It helps to have some added advice in your corner!

So we start right here with a look at a few basics that can help get you up and running with the minimum of fuss. This is the chapter you need if you've never tried *Minecraft* before!

What we're going to do, then, is start off by explaining just where Minecraft came from, and how it grew to be the game that it is today. Then we're going to explore how the various versions differ, so you can be sure just what

you're dealing with! Or you could simply start getting your hands dirty and flick over to our guide to the very basics of the game. We've followed that up with a list of tips to help you get started as quickly and easily as possible.

We've just left ourselves room in this chapter to go through a special toolkit for first-time or inexperienced Minecraft players. And we're going to be having a chat about mobs as well!

If all goes to plan, by the time you've worked your way through this chapter, you'll have everything you need to be fully up and running, and be ready to tackle some of the more advanced tips and tricks we're going to be talking about later. It's time to get to work...

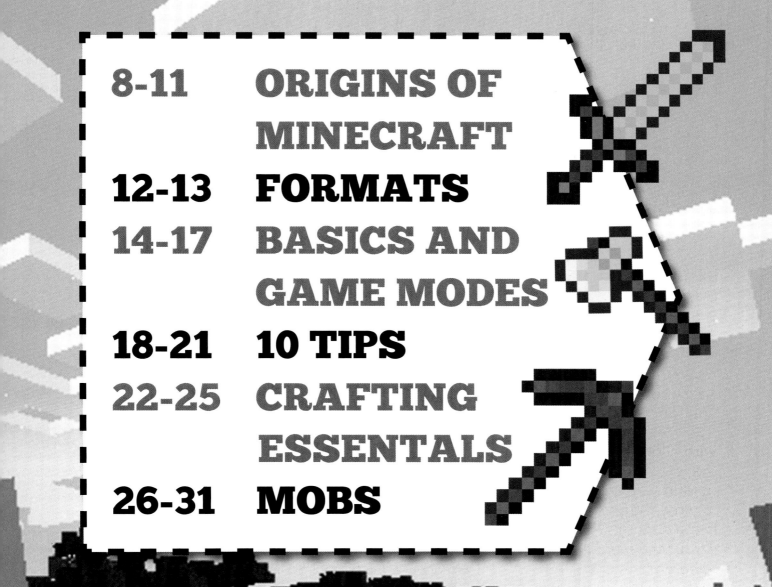

8-11	ORIGINS OF MINECRAFT
12-13	FORMATS
14-17	BASICS AND GAME MODES
18-21	10 TIPS
22-25	CRAFTING ESSENTALS
26-31	MOBS

THE BASICS

THE STORY OF MINECRAFT

Minecraft is a gaming phenomenon. There's no other way to put it. From humble beginnings, the creator and developer of the project, Markus 'Notch' Persson, has turned Minecraft from a small side project into a virtual industry in its own right. But where did it come from? And how has it affected the world around it? Before you start playing, it's worth learning the story of Minecraft, the people behind it, and how one game managed to conquer the world...!

PREPARING FOR THE WITHER BEGINNINGS

Minecraft was initially developed by programmer Markus Persson as a side project while he was working full time as a games developer in Sweden. In its earliest form, the game was inspired by the Zachtronic Industries game 'Infiniminer', which had recently been discontinued. Persson took the basic mechanics of Infiniminer – mining resources in a randomly generated world – and planned to add RPG elements. Along the way, the game turned into an open-world sandbox, where there were no particular goals and no narrative thread. With such an unconventional formula, it's fair to say that no-one could have predicted the popularity to follow.

The first developmental alpha version of Minecraft was released on 17th May 2009. At the time, Persson was still in full-time work, but by June the game had become so popular that he quit work to devote himself to

Zachtronic Industries' Infiniminer – the game that inspired Minecraft

Minecraft's five GDC awards received in 2011

the project full time. As the game grew in popularity, Mojang (Persson's company) began to fund development by charging for downloads, with the promise of free lifetime updates for all buyers. The model was a hit, and Minecraft received hundreds of thousands of downloads even before reaching its beta release in December 2010. In January 2011, it hit one million purchases, despite no commercial advertising or publisher backing. The game's 'full' release (i.e. non-beta) followed less than a year later, in November 2011.

It's hard to overstate the success that Minecraft enjoys, even so long after its initial release. When the Xbox 360 version was launched, its massive popularity ensured that it became profitable within 24 hours of release. Further milestones have been reached, too. The PC version, for instance, had 100 million registered users by February 2014 (adding even more in 2015!), and it's hit big on Xbox One and PlayStation 4 as well.

Since Minecraft's full release, Persson has moved onto new projects, but development of Minecraft has continued under the auspices of the game's second lead designer, Jens 'Jeb' Bergensten, with new features and mechanics being added constantly at no extra cost to customers.

Persson has stated that lawyers have officially advised him that he should no longer promise to deliver all future updates for free, but so far no version of Minecraft has charged for updates.

ACCLAIM & APPEAL

Minecraft's reception has been incredible even at the most conservative estimates.

A Lego Minecraft set

The PC version aggregates over 90%, and received 9/10 from *Edge* magazine, 10/10 from Eurogamer and 9/10 from IGN. In 2010, PC gaming website Rock, Paper, Shotgun named it game of the year, and in March 2011, while still technically in its beta stage, Minecraft received five awards at GDC, the Game Developers Conference. As well as the Innovation award, Best Downloadable Game award and Best Debut Game award from the Game Developer's Choice Awards, the Independent Games Festival also awarded it the Audience Choice award and the Seumas McNally Grand Prize. In 2015, meanwhile, the console versions of the game won the prestigious Best Family Game BAFTA.

However, perhaps the most palpable acclaim comes from its loyal fanbase and devoted players everywhere. The PC version alone has sold over 19 million copies, and combined sales of all platforms are believed to top 60 million. To put that in context, on the Xbox 360, Call of Duty: Modern Warfare sold 7.5 million copies – Minecraft sold 7 million. On the PC, Minecraft is the now best-selling game of all time, beating the likes of The Sims 3, World Of Warcraft, Diablo 3 and Half Life 2. Huge numbers for any game, let alone a title that began as the pet project of one man.

It's hard to explain where Minecraft's appeal comes from. Each player takes something different from the experience. Some enjoy the rewards of exploration and discovery. Others favour the problem-solving of staying alive and defending yourself. Some follow the game's secrets to reach the end game, while others are content to simply build a world for themselves.

Perhaps it's the simplicity that appeals. The core mechanic of breaking blocks, collecting them and using them to build something else recalls the simplest childhood toys, while allowing the imagination to run wild with possibilities. The game's visuals are deliberately understated, avoiding any kind of graphical arms race and allowing the distinctive look to define the game.

Although the game looks simple and is undoubtedly easy to pick up, the depth and complexity of the engine actually run further than anyone would expect simply from looking at it. The game's built-in system of circuitry (redstone) has been used to create incredibly complicated machinery, including working computer processors, although admittedly ones that take up large sections of landscape!

Most versions of Minecraft have a multiplayer mode, which allows players to invite their friends into their world for collaboration, co-operative play, or even a deathmatch-style fight. An industry has grown around providing persistent multiplayer servers that allow for the creation of long-running worlds with their own modifications and rule sets.

Indeed, the 'modding' community around the game gives it a substantial portion of its appeal and longevity. Variations on Minecraft allow users everywhere to exercise their creative freedom to even greater degrees. Whether adding new textures, new tools, new blocks and even entirely new landscapes, Minecraft's ability to entertain stretches far beyond the confines of the game's world. Unlicensed mods inspired by the likes of Pokemon, Portal and Star Trek are available, as well as hundreds of other

A life-size foam Minecraft pickaxe!

Minecraft
Easter egg from
Borderlands 2

19 Creeper

community-led projects based around the game's engine. Indeed, recent releases have incorporated extra support for modding to accommodate the unexpected popularity of the practice.

MINECRAFT IN THE REAL WORLD

Further evidence of the game's community can be found in the shape of the annual 'Minecon' convention, which brings together fans across the globe. The 2011 convention was held in Las Vegas, while the 2012 gathering took place in Disneyland Paris. Minecon 2015, the most recent, was held in London. Conventions involve a number of panels and discussions, as well as talks from developers and musical guests.

Minecraft has also proven popular with merchandisers. Given that the game shares much of its appeal with building blocks, it may come as no surprise that in 2012 Lego released the first official Minecraft tie-in set. Comprised of four 'chunks', it also contained Lego models of the player and a creeper. Sets are

compatible with official Lego and can be expanded or augmented using it.

Other official Minecraft merchandise includes a wide variety of T-shirts, life-size foam pickaxes and swords, Minecraft block magnets and toys of the game's monsters.

THE FUTURE

Minecraft continues to be hugely popular across more platforms than ever, and it's now part of the Microsoft empire. The company bought Mojang for an incredible $2.5bn, completing the deal at the end of 2014. Microsoft is, as you might expect, heavily supporting the game, although Markus Persson left when the takeover was complete. Rumours continue to circle about a possible Minecraft 2 (at one stage it was even announced as an April Fools' joke!), but more likely you'll see a continued expansion of the game over the years to come. There's even a major Hollywood movie being planned from some of the people behind *The Lego Movie*.

With Minecraft now even being taught in schools, it's become a gaming phenomenon like no other. Its story is only really just getting started...

Minecon 2011

MINECON

Block by Block's recreation of a village's open space in Minecraft

UNDUGU PLAYGROUND

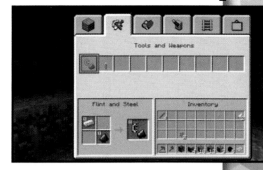

Minecraft's popularity has seen it spread beyond the PC onto a wide variety of systems, including games consoles, tablets and smartphones. Each version is different, however. The bulk of this guide uses the PC version as reference, but in case you're playing on a different format (or plan to) here's a breakdown of each one.

PC MINECRAFT

The PC version contains the most advanced feature set and graphics of any release. It's available for Windows, Mac OS X and Linux. Major updates are released every two months, and bug fixes and tweaks more frequently. Unless stated, all content in this guide refers primarily to features in PC version 1.8.6. If you're playing a newer version (or one on another platform), some blocks and features may be unavailable or behave differently!

The PC version is the only one to feature Minecraft Realms, the subscription-based service that lets players create and manage their own servers hosted by Mojang.

XBOX AND PLAYSTATION EDITIONS

The Xbox and PlayStation Editions are the second most 'complete' versions of the game and are in constant development, with regular updates. The original base for the Xbox 360 version was the PC release 1.6.6, although recent updates have added features introduced since then, and the Xbox One and PS4 versions have enhanced it further, with larger worlds.

HOW FORMATS DIFFER

Perhaps the largest difference in the console editions is the interface, which is optimised for a controller. In particular, crafting is performed through a series of menus that allow players to directly select the items they want to craft from available resources, rather than learning the patterns and recipes for each.

The console versions feature both an online multiplayer mode (with one player hosting the game's world) and a split-screen mode for up to four players. Using two consoles in split screen allows eight players to enter a single world. There's also a unique tutorial mode, and players are automatically given a map at the start of a game. Xbox 360 and PS3 worlds are limited to 864 x 864 blocks and surrounded by sea, and the Nether is correspondingly smaller. The Xbox One and PS4 worlds, however, are around 36 times larger.

The game contains a number of default player skins, and additional skin packs can be purchased as DLC. The console versions are also the only ones to have physical releases, and boxed copies are available at retail stores and via the platform's digital store.

MINECRAFT POCKET EDITION (IOS & ANDROID)

Smartphones and tablets have their own dedicated release known as Pocket Edition. First made available exclusively on Android in August 2011, an iOS version was released in November the same year.

Although the game is similar to early incarnations of the PC version, it lacks many features found in both it and the Xbox 360 version – in particular, the ability to create redstone circuits and minecart rail systems. The local multiplayer features are compatible between iOS and Android, but not with any other version, but a future update will give players the chance to buy a persistent online 'realm' using an in-app purchase.

The interface for the Pocket Edition has been adapted for a touch interface, and the graphical complexity of the game reduced to allow for the weaker processing capabilities of portable devices. The worlds generated are finite in size, and the terrain is missing many biomes.

Although the Pocket Edition doesn't contain the Nether, players can build the 'Nether reactor', a structure that generates Netherrack and spawns zombie pigmen. Other unique features include the stone cutter block, blue roses and glowing obsidian.

RASPBERRY PI MINECRAFT

Although leaked in December 2012, the official Raspberry Pi release was available in February 2013. Its block set is equivalent to Pocket Edition 0.5.0, and it can run in Creative mode only, with no mobs (passive or hostile) and no crafting or smelting. Since the Pi is a learning aid for programming, users are encouraged to modify the game's code to make alterations. It has remained on version 0.1.1 for a while, but is still in active development.

THE BASICS AND GAME MODES

So, what's Minecraft all about, and what are the available game modes? Read on to find out

Minecraft is a game about blocks. More specifically, it's about building things out of these blocks, which are made up of all sorts of materials. Blocks of ore, gemstones and other rare materials are mined by digging deep into the game world, and other materials can be gathered by making the most of the flora and fauna around you.

These items are then used to create tools, structures, contraptions and weapons, which you can use, depending on the game mode you're playing in, to thrive and survive a harsh world. If you're not into the whole survival thing, you can simply use Minecraft to create anything your mind can imagine.

The world you play in is generated by entering a seed code, or using a random string of characters. No two codes will generate the same world, making each player's experience unique. On the Xbox 360 and PS3, this world, although still large, is limited in size. Xbox One and PS4 worlds are even larger, but not infinite. The PC version, on the other hand, will generate new areas of the world as you explore, making for an almost endless environment in each and every game.

Worlds are split into various environment types, or 'biomes'. These include forest, flatland, jungle, swamp, ocean and more. Each biome is home to different creatures and foliage, and you'll need to explore them all in order to find the essential resources to progress in the game.

As you explore the world, you'll also meet enemies, or 'mobs'. These creatures come in all shapes and sizes. All are dangerous, but some are far more troublesome than others, with one of the most feared being the iconic creeper.

Most, but not all, enemies come out at night

Minecraft's world is split into many different environmental biomes

time, and to defend yourself against attacks you'll need to fashion weapons and build secure structures to take shelter in. These structures will also hold your supply chests, where you'll store all of your gathered items and resources, and you'll also need a bed to sleep in, to fast forward time to the next morning. Other essential equipment to keep safe in your home includes crafting tables, furnaces, brewing stands, enchantment tables and more.

You're about to embark upon an epic quest in an always dangerous and unique world

Singleplayer

Multiplayer

Options...   Quit Game

Minecraft 1.6.2   Copyright Mo.iang AB. Do not distribute!

That only scratches the surface of Minecraft's world, however, and below the picturesque vistas you'll find a network of caves, tunnels, mines and strongholds. Infested with monsters, saturated with underground waterways, burnt by lakes of lava and plagued with precarious footholds, these locations are where you'll find the most valuable and rarest loot.

Eventually, you'll leave the game's Overworld and venture into the alternate dimension of the Nether, a dark, foreboding world that's home to even more dangerous foes. Then, if you survive, you may be lucky enough to enter the End, the realm of the game's major foe, the ender dragon.

Minecraft is playable alone or with friends. Players host their own worlds if playing online, and others can join in to help survive and defeat foes, or simply to build new structures and sculpt new worlds. Console owners can also play with up to three friends in split screen.

When playing online, it's always advisable to play with friends you know, as griefing (the act of ruining another's world or cheating) is possible. Some game modes, such as Adventure, can prevent this, but for the best possible experiences only allow those you know into the game, otherwise all your hard work could be undone.

If you're a PC user, there are ways to further expand the game, such as new player skins, world textures and other modifications. Console players can also use skins, but from a list available on XBLA and PSN. Texture support is included too, with new packs available for purchase.

Minecraft can be a simple creation tool, or a deep, complex adventure game. Modes differ greatly, and we'll explain their features and differences here.

CREATIVE

As the title suggests, Creative mode is just that, a mode that simply lets you play around with the game world, building anything you like without restriction. Unlike other modes, there are no enemies and no need to go mining for resources. In this mode, you're given unlimited access to all the different resources you need to build your world.

Creative mode replaces the usual inventory menu system with a selection screen containing all of the game's available items in one place, and you have unlimited access to them. The world is yours to sculpt, and you have no life bar and can't die (unless you use the /kill console command or go too deep into the void, past -64 y coordinates). You can fly in Creative mode too (double-tap jump and use jump and sneak to ascend and descend). Enemy mobs will still spawn here, but they're always passive and won't harm you if you leave them alone. Just beware of the always terrifying creepers. Although they're not a threat to you, they can still explode and damage your creations.

SURVIVAL

This is the main 'game' mode, and is the one you'll be playing if you want to experience all it has to offer. Here, you're dropped into a new world with nothing but the will to survive.

You'll have to gather materials, build a home to shelter you from the night and the things that come out to play, and farm, mine and quest for rare ore and materials to help get you to the Nether and, ultimately, to the End and a battle with the ender dragon.

Hardcore mode is the steepest challenge on offer in Minecraft

Unlike Creative mode, Survival worlds are very dangerous places. You'll have few friends, and you'll have to manage your health and hunger levels. Nothing is given to you here, and you have to gather everything. It's all out there in the world, you just have to work for it.

As you mine certain materials and kill certain mobs, you'll earn experience which can be used to enchant items when you have an enchanting table. You'll also need to keep

yourself fed, otherwise you'll be unable to heal.

Much of this guide will focus on the methods and tactics you need to employ in Survival. Although there's no set way to 'win' Minecraft, there are some staple things you need to do in order to reach the End and beat the ender dragon, the game's main boss. Let's start with the basics:

1 Arrive in your world, build basic tools and equipment, and establish a home base. Mine resources and gather basic, early supplies such as food, weapons and simple armour so you can explore the world relatively safely.

2 Mine more valuable and rare minerals in order to make stronger tools and better equipment, including more durable armour and stronger swords. Eventually locate diamonds. With diamond pickaxe in hand, find obsidian.

3 Build a portal to the Nether, a hellish place that's home to essential materials, such as blaze rods.

4 Find and kill endermen to collect ender pearls. Construct an eye of ender, which can be used to locate a stronghold.

5 With 12 eyes of ender in your possession (although you may not need 12, as some may be already in place), enter the stronghold and open a portal to the End, where you'll do battle with the ender dragon.

6 If you're feeling brave, build and take on Minecraft's second boss, the wither.

Of course, there's a lot more to beating Survival than that, but that's what the rest of this handy guide is for.

HARDCORE

Hardcore mode is a brutal variant of Survival and features the same gameplay, with a big difference – you get one life. Rather than the option to respawn indefinitely, Hardcore gives you a solitary chance to survive through your quest. If you die, that's it, the game-over screen appears. It goes without saying that this isn't a mode for beginners, and even the most experienced players can easily fall to this steep challenge.

ADVENTURE

This PC mode is designed to make the most out of player-created worlds. It functions similarly to Survival mode, except that players are unable to destroy blocks.

The aim here isn't to build (you can't actually place blocks), but instead to explore other players' worlds, gather food to stay healthy and craft items to help you survive. There's more of an emphasis on exploration, as you need to find safe places to hide for the night.

The command block, unique to Adventure mode, can be used by map creators to interact with players and perform specific tasks, such as granting experience to players, or providing items.

Adventure mode isn't accessible from the mode select, but is accessed from the chat window (with cheats enabled). Press T to open this, then type '/gamemode 2'. This will change the game type to Adventure.

As previously stated, in this mode players can't place or destroy blocks. Before the 1.8 updates, it was possible to destroy blocks in Adventure, and most of the time you needed the correct tool for the job, which isn't a rule in other modes. As this feature has been removed, some Adventure players run servers using pre-1.8 versions of Minecraft. If you play on there, you'll need to know which tools are right for the job. Below you'll find a list of tools needed for reference.

Using the CanDestroy command, server admins can still allow items to destroy blocks in 1.8 and later, but this is determined by the server operator. Items and their uses can change from server to server.

DESTROYABLE WITH ANYTHING

All plants, crops and mushrooms (not including pumpkins, melons and trees)
Beacons
Buttons
Carpets
Comparators
Flower pots
Glass blocks/panes
Glowstone
Heads
Ice and packed ice
Ladders
Levers
Snow
Paintings and item frames
Pots
Rails
Redstone dust trails
Redstone lamps
Redstone torches
Repeaters
Tripwire hooks
Vines

WITH AXES

Bookshelves
Chests
Crafting tables
Daylight sensors
Fences (wood)
Fence gates
Huge mushrooms
Jack 'o' lanterns
Jukeboxes
Note blocks
Planks
Pumpkins
Signs
Trap chests
Trap doors (wood)

Wood
Wooden doors
Wood pressure plates
Wood slabs/stairs

WITH PICKAXES

All ores (wooden pickaxes will break ores, but you may not gather any resources)
All resource and mineral blocks
Cobblestone blocks
Dispensers/droppers
Enchantment tables
Ender chests
Furnaces
Hardened/stained clay
Hoppers
Iron bars and doors
Monster spawners
Nether bricks/fences
Obsidian
Stone and stone bricks
Sandstone

WITH SHOVELS

Dirt
Grass blocks
Gravel
Sand

WITH SHEARS

All leaves and wool
Cobwebs
Melons and pumpkins

WITH SWORDS

All leaves
Cobwebs
Jack 'o' lanterns
Enemies!

The initial stages of a Minecraft game are rich with possibility, but actually taking those first steps can be daunting, especially if you're worried about taking them in the wrong direction! To help get you started, we've compiled a list of ten hints that should be useful to any Minecraft newbie. Ignore them at your peril!

WOOD YOU LIKE TO BEGIN?

Few things in Minecraft are your friends unconditionally, but trees definitely are. It's a bitter irony that you're destined to spend the rest of the game hacking them down! From the very moment you enter your world, all of your initial thoughts should be focussed on finding and tearing down the nearest piece of topiary. Luckily, there are no environmental consequences to deforestation in Minecraft.

You can mine tree blocks reasonably fast using only your hands, and a few good pieces of timber will provide you with most of the raw materials you need to get started. Turn wood blocks into planks, turn a few planks into sticks, and before you know it you can have a crafting table, spade, sword

A new world to explore! Infinite possibilities open up before you! Er, what now?

and pick ready to take on a search for stone, coal, or whatever else it is that you desire!

DON'T STRAY TOO FAR

The world of Minecraft is huge. On the PC, it will generate new terrain for as long as you're walking towards the edges of the map, and even on the console's limited-size lands it's easy to get lost. That's why one of the first things you should do in any Minecraft game is decide on the place you're going to call home and spend time getting to know it.

10 TIPS FOR GETTING STARTED

This doesn't necessarily mean creating your own shelter or cave, although that is a good idea. It could be that you simply build a small tower of blocks, or find a prominent landmark that you'll be able to recognise from far away. Anything to help you figure out which way you're going and how to get back is essential for taming your newborn

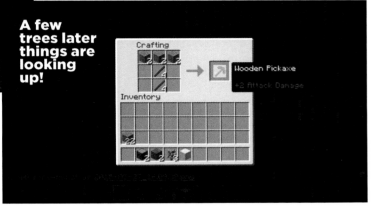

A few trees later things are looking up!

world. Later on you'll have maps and compasses, and all sorts of ways to get back to where you want to be, but until then you have to get the lay of the land.

KEEP IT SIMPLE

You begin Minecraft much the same way an infant begins its life: a mewling speck in a vast, mostly hostile world, completely lacking any key knowledge, skills or tools. That's why it's a bad idea to run headlong into the first cave you find and try to beat a path to some of the rarer minerals and metals, unless your goal is to scare the living daylights out of yourself during a particularly nasty spider attack.

To begin with, keep your goals small. Planning to stay alive is a good start. Your first actions should be defensive and preparatory. Build tools, shelter and try to locate some food. If there's time, maybe craft some armour. Learn the basics. From the very moment you start playing, the clock begins ticking towards nightfall, and there

are few things more terrifying than your first night in Minecraft. Expect to spend it shivering and lonely at the absolute best. If you make it to the following dawn alive, only then can you start getting ambitious.

BUNKER DOWN

To maximise your chances of making it to the following day alive, forgo the spirit of pioneering adventure in favour of a little house-building. Again, don't be too ambitious. In time, you may come to construct the kind of architectural miracles that would make Kevin McCloud fall to his knees, but for day one it doesn't matter if you construct a mud hut without a proper door as long as the mobs can't get in when night falls. It's either that or climb to the top of a tree and hope our simian ancestors were right about the protective qualities a tall branch can provide...!

LET THERE BE LIGHT

Once you've got your tools together, the next thing to do is go looking for coal. Coal helps you make torches, and you can never

It's not much, but it's home. Sort of. Bring on the night!

have too many torches. As well as lighting the way ahead, they serve a vital defensive purpose: most mobs only spawn in the dark. If you want to remain safe overnight, the best way to do this is to knock together enough torches that there isn't a nook or cranny within your preferred shelter that remains in shadow. This applies whether you've walled yourself into an existing cave, constructed a makeshift shack or carved out a hidey hole in a cliff. Either way, a few torches will increase your chances of surviving to the following day.

Charcoal is easy to make. Unfortunately, Minecraft doesn't support barbecues. Yet.

When you're exploring, torches are also a good way to lay down some tracks. They remain visible even at a great distance, especially at night, so placing a few torches as you wander around will make it easy to find your way back home if you get lost before you've found the resources to craft more conventional pathfinding tools.

ALTERNATIVE FUEL

Although it's normally easy to find coal without venturing too far from the surface, there's always a chance you'll run out or fail to find any. The good news is that if you've got a furnace (and by the time you've got a pick and a crafting table, there's no impediment to crafting one – stone is in abundant supply) you can smelt wood to turn it into charcoal, which works in much the same way as coal and can be used for most of the same things.

Bunnies may be cute, but when it's death from starvation, or a cuddly friend, there's only one option...

To create a piece of charcoal, simply 'smelt' wood in a furnace. Although it might sound counter-intuitive to burn something without coal to use as fuel, remember that furnaces can use wood, planks, saplings, lava buckets, sticks and even wooden tools as their fuel source, although these are less efficient than coal or charcoal!

PEACE IN OUR TIME

If you're struggling to get started due to the zombie hordes closing in on you, a quick poke around in Minecraft's difficulty settings should allow you access to the difficulty settings. Set the game to Peaceful mode for a few sessions and you'll be able to learn the ropes at your own pace.

In Peaceful mode, mobs won't spawn at all, allowing you to roam the game's landscape free from its more terrifying quirks. The food bar won't deplete, meaning your chances of starving to death underground are greatly reduced. And if you do injure yourself, you'll gradually regain health without any intervention.

Of course, there are things you can't do in Peaceful mode – some items are only obtainable by killing mobs – but if you're trying to get started, it might offer the helping hand you need.

DINING FOR ONE

On any difficulty mode other than Peaceful, you'll notice that the more time you spend in your world, the more your food bar depletes. If the food bar empties completely, you'll start to lose health. On higher difficulty levels, this can lead to you starving to death!

The good news is that food isn't hard to come by. Later in the game you can actively farm food or follow recipes, but when you're still in the early moment of an adventure, the quickest thing to do is find and kill some animals. Do it with your bare hands if you're feeling particularly Chuck Norris, but a few whacks to the head with even a wooden sword is quicker. Cows, pigs, sheep, rabbits, chickens and fish are good sources of food. Remember that you can find food in other ways too: oak tree leaves have a 0.5% chance of dropping an apple when they decay or are destroyed, so you can pick up food while gathering wood.

You can drown in a teaspoon of water. Or, in this case, several metres of water.

Fully skeleton-resistant! But that wooden door can be bashed down by zombies

BED DOWN

If you survive long enough to encounter a few sheep, do your best to kill them and take the wool that they drop. Three blocks of wool (any colour) combined with three planks will make a bed, and these will significantly improve your time in the world of Minecraft. Sleeping in a bed allows you to skip nights (as long as they're placed in a safe, well-lit location!) and also resets your spawn point, meaning that if you die you return to the bed you last slept in instead of the place you started the game.

Don't worry if you can't craft a bed straight away – they're convenient, but not essential. Still, they'll help you avoid a lot of waiting around and stop you having to retrace too many steps when you die, so

Beds are optional, but they're comfy, and also reset your spawn point

it's a smart move to build one as soon as possible.

DON'T WORRY IF YOU DIE

Here's the thing about Minecraft: there are lots of ways to die, and even if you're playing in Peaceful mode, where there aren't any mobs to hunt you down in the dead of night, you're not going to live forever. Eventually, you'll fall into some lava or mistime a jump and drop off a cliff, or stand too close to some falling gravel. But here's the good thing: it doesn't matter.

That's not to say there aren't consequences. But they're weighted such that dying only hurts when you've been playing a long time. Losing your stuff can be annoying, but it's easy to replace, particularly in the early stages of the game. Losing experience barely has any effect until you've been adventuring for days. And losing your place? That's just part of the fun!

So don't be shy. If you find yourself on the business end of a skeleton arrow, dust yourself off, cut down another tree and start again. Eventually, you'll forget dying was ever a problem! Well, unless you're playing on Hardcore mode – that's a different story though!

CRAFTING ESSENTIALS

The basic four tools - sword, pickaxe, axe and shovel. Stone and iron tools are suitable for most tasks

Minecraft allows players to create hundreds of different items. It's all part of the fun! But if you're just getting started, it can be tough to tell the practical items from the decorative ones, or the necessary from the optional. Resources may take a while to gather, so using your hard-won materials up on items that turn out to be pointless, ineffective or simply used for something different than you thought can be frustrating and time consuming.

In this part of the guide, we'll point you in the direction of the items you simply can't do without, highlighting their advantages, disadvantages, quirks and special qualities. Recipes for each item can be found in the glossary at the back of this guide, but they can only tell you how to make each tool. Keep reading to learn why you might want to!

MATERIAL PROPERTIES

The basic tools and armour come in several varieties depending on what material they're crafted from. An item's durability determines how many times it can be used before it breaks, while its speed (where applicable) refers to the time it takes to mine a block, relative to other tools.

Wooden tools are weak with low durability, but easy to create due to the abundance of their raw materials. Most players start off using these, but quickly upgrade.

Stone tools are more than twice as durable as wooden ones, and almost twice as fast. Although stone is abundant, it's rare to be in a situation where cobblestone is readily available, but iron ore isn't, so don't expect to use them as much more than a stepping stone (excuse the pun) to greater things, although they're easy to make if you're underground and in a fix!

Iron tools are the ones you'll use most frequently, at least for the bulk of your playing time. They're almost twice as durable as stone tools and 30% faster. Iron ore is much less abundant than wood or stone, but still fairly easy to come by, making iron tools a staple of any adventurer's inventory.

Gold tools are a special case. As in real life, Minecraft's gold is incredibly soft, meaning tools made with gold have high speed but low durability. Gold tools are actually half as durable as wooden ones, meaning they break quicker than almost any other item in the game – but they're also the fastest by some distance. Because gold is rare, it makes more sense to use it on other things than for tool crafting. Gold's real benefit is the readiness with which it accepts enchantment, but you'll find more details on that in the Advanced section of the guide!

Diamond tools are much sought after due to their high durability (more than 25 times as durable as wooden tools) and speed (more than five times quicker than wooden tools). However, diamond ore is incredibly rare and difficult to find in high quantities, so finding enough to make them requires a huge time investment, not to mention a significant amount of raw materials. They're not the only use for diamond, either, so think hard before you commit those precious rocks!

PICKAXES

If you consider that the game is called Minecraft, it probably won't surprise you to learn that pickaxes are the most essential tool you'll encounter. You can try playing without a pickaxe, but you won't get very far. At the best, you'll get there very slowly, until you hit obsidian, where you'll stop.

A wooden pickaxe is probably the first item most players will create using their crafting table. They're not much use long term, though. Wooden pickaxes can only be used to mine cobblestone and coal. Use them on anything harder, such as iron ore or redstone, and they'll simply destroy the resource instead of collecting it.

The good news is that once you've mined some cobblestone, you can create a stone pick! Stone picks are more durable and can be used to acquire metals and minerals, most significantly iron ore, which can be used to create the type of pickaxe you'll spend much of your time with: the iron pickaxe. Notably, stone pickaxes *can't* mine rare metals or gems, so don't use them on diamond ore, emerald ore or gold ore. For those blocks, use an iron pickaxe or better.

Diamond pickaxes are the only type that can mine the super-hard blocks of obsidian you'll find wherever still lava and water meet. Other tools can destroy obsidian blocks, but it takes a lot of time and you'll lose any resources. For this reason, and the importance of the pickaxe, this is the first diamond item you'll want to craft.

SHOVELS

Although it wouldn't halt your progress in the game to ignore shovels, it would be an oversight that could potentially cost a lot of time. Shovels are almost as useful as pickaxes, and it's worth keeping at least one in your inventory at all times. They tend to last longer than pickaxes because you won't use them as frequently, but there are enough situations that demand one to make them a mainstay of anyone's inventory.

Shovels can be crafted out of wood, stone, iron, gold or diamond, although aside from the usual speed and durability constraints associated with each material, there are no special factors involved in their use. That said, shovels (of any material) are the only item in the game that can be used to collect snow in the form of snowballs. Any other tool (or bare hands) will simply destroy the snow block, dropping nothing. Other than that, shovels simply speed up the process of mining softer blocks – dirt, gravel, sand, clay and snow are all harvested near instantly by a shovel. Stone and iron are best for shovels. Diamonds aren't worth wasting on them.

AXES

Unlike all other tools, axes are good for at least two uses. As well as mining wood and wood-related blocks with great speed, an axe can do almost as much damage as a sword (just half a heart less than a sword crafted with equivalent material), making them a decent choice of offensive weapon if a sword is unavailable for any reason. There are some disadvantages, though – unlike swords, axes can't be used to parry an attack, and when used as a weapon the axe will lose two durability points, not one.

The primary use of an axe is to mine wood-based blocks, including wood (tree trunks), wooden planks, and furniture such as chests and bookshelves. Axes destroy these blocks quicker than any other and, while they aren't mandatory (again, there are no blocks they can mine that bare hands can't also), they're worth using due to the speed with which they work.

Although it may seem counter-intuitive, axes shouldn't be used to destroy leaf blocks. Leaves are easily destroyed by bare hands, so using an axe will cause it to lose durability to no particular benefit! Again, don't waste diamonds, and stick to stone or iron.

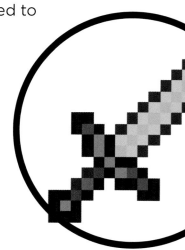

SWORDS

Swords are melee weapons designed to cause damage to mobs and players, which can be used to 'parry' or defend against an attack from the same. Again, there are no special qualities possessed by swords of different materials, besides the speed and durability of the material.

All swords do share some advantageous behaviour, however. They can destroy cobwebs quicker than any other tool (turning them into string), while boats and minecarts attacked with a sword will be destroyed quickly and without any cost to the sword's durability. That said, when a sword is used on any block that isn't instantly destroyed, its durability is decreased by 2 instead of 1 when the block is destroyed. Swords are good for short-range combat and (appearances aside) can't reach further than any other handheld tool when attacking. Parries will block projectiles, but cause the player to move much slower than even sneaking allows. As swords are so essential, it's well worth having a diamond one, especially for boss fights.

ARMOUR

Armour is slightly different to the basic tools in that it can't be made from wood or stone, but can be crafted from leather (which is most easily obtained by killing cows or horses). It's also possible to obtain rare (though unspectacular) 'chain' armour, but only through trading or mob drops. Armour comes in four parts – headgear, chestpiece, leggings and boots – and will absorb damage before the player's health is affected. It protects against most direct attacks – such as weapons, projectiles, fire and lava – but not more passive injuries, like those obtained by drowning, starving or poisoning.

Early in the game, it's likely that you'll quickly find yourself wearing leather armour, simply because it's possible to find leather without venturing too far below ground where attacking mobs can make mincemeat out of an unprotected player. Cows are easy to find, so take your sword and set to work!

As you'd expect, leather armour is the weakest and least protective, although leather boots are as protective as gold and chain boots, so bear that in mind when crafting full suits. Leather also has the property unique amongst armour that it can be dyed, so if you want to create colourful outfits it's the best way to do so.

Although diamond armour is the most protective (followed by iron, chain, gold, then leather), a full set of diamond armour is hard to get due to the rarity of the gems.

You'll spend most of your time wearing iron armour (if any). Iron is easy to obtain and provides the second strongest protection – only a shade lower than diamond – although, admittedly, it's just under half as durable! Diamond armour is only really needed when fighting the ender dragon and wither, so save it for these confrontations.

MOBS

Minecraft's many dangers often pale in comparison to the game's variety of enemies, or 'mobs'. Here's what you're up against.

PASSIVE MOBS

These creatures will never attack you, and can be farmed, tamed and are useful for many tasks.

Bats: Bats are one of the few flying mobs, and if killed don't drop anything at all. They spawn in darker areas, and if you find them out in the world they can often signify a nearby cave. Bats emit a squeaking noise.

Chickens: Chickens are a source of food, eggs (to breed more chickens and cook with) and feathers, which you'll need to make arrows. Drawn to light sources, they can be found wandering the world and can be lured with wheat and melon seeds. They can become an infinite source of valuable resources.

Cows: Cows are a source of leather, beef and milk (by using a bucket), and can be farmed for a renewable source of these resources. They spawn in various locations. As they're the only source of milk (along with mooshrooms), cows are very useful, more so than other livestock like pigs, as they provide more resources.

Mooshrooms: Mooshrooms are a hybrid cow/ mushroom mob that can be found wandering around mushroom biomes. Although they look odd, mooshrooms are very useful.

Mooshrooms share a lot in common with normal cows, and can be slaughtered for leather and beef. They can also be milked using a bucket. You can also use shears to shave off their mushrooms (which turns them into a normal cow), and you can use empty wooden bowls to milk them for an inexhaustible supply of mushroom soup. If you capture one, this makes for the only food supply you'll need. They only spawn in mushroom biomes.

Horses: A tameable creature that you can ride around and clad in armour. They spawn on plains biomes and can also wander into other areas. You can ride horses right away, but they're tricky to control. Ideally, you need to saddle them. Horses come in different varieties. Aside from normal horses, you can find donkeys and mules. Skeleton and zombie horses are featured, but aren't spawned in normal gameplay.

Ocelots: The second tameable mob in the game, ocelots are native to jungle biomes and can be tamed by using raw fish. They're shy and will run away from you. Once tamed, ocelots become cats and can follow you. Cats are the only creature that can scare away creepers.

Pigs: Pigs, like cows and chickens, are a good source of food, dropping porkchops if killed. They don't drop anything else, but if you manage to place a saddle on one you can use a carrot and a stick to ride them around. They spawn in various locations. Once they speed up, pigs can be an effective way to get around, and they can jump, climb stairs and even ladders. Carrots only last so long, though, so pack a good supply.

Rabbits: Rabbits are a more recent addition, and if killed will drop rabbit hide and raw rabbit. They'll also rarely drop a rabbit's foot, which can be used in potion brewing. Beware killer bunnies. There are white with red eyes and will attack on sight. They also attack wolves.

Sheep: Sheep are mainly used as a source of wool, which can be dyed and used for various tasks. They can also drop raw mutton, which is a good foodstuff. They can be found all around the Overworld. If sheep are killed, they'll drop blocks of wool, but a far better method is to use shears on them. This grants more wool and doesn't kill the sheep. Then, when the sheep eats some grass, its wool grows back. For this reason, it's a good idea to capture and breed sheep.

Squid: Squid are found only in water and, although they can look fairly threatening, they're harmless. If killed, they drop ink sacs, which can be used to create dyes. Ink can also be used to craft books and quills.

Villagers: Villager mobs can be found in NPC villages where they wander inside and outside of buildings. They each have their own roles, such as blacksmith, and players can trade with them. They don't attack the player, but will run into their homes to escape zombies.

Villagers will breed depending on the number of doors in the village, and baby villagers can be found playing around. Villager professions are as follows:
● Blacksmith ● Butcher ● Farmer ● Librarian
● Priest ● Villager

Using a villager will cause the trading screen to appear, and you can swap goods with them. The trades offered will depend upon their chosen profession. Villagers can also become zombies (see Zombie mob entry).

NEUTRAL MOBS

Neutral mobs are unique in that they won't attack you unless provoked.

Endermen: Endermen are tall, dark humanoids with glowing purple eyes. They're found all around the Overworld and in the End. They're fond of teleporting around, and picking up and moving random blocks, including your structures. They're vulnerable to water, and take damage from both bodies of water and rain.

Endermen can be provoked in two ways. The first is to attack them, and the second is to simply look at them (place the cross-hairs over them), or at least their upper body. Doing so from within a 64-block radius will cause them to shake then attack you until you kill them or they kill you. They can't see through transparent blocks such as glass.

Avoiding them is easy enough, but unfortunately

Beware the endermen...!

you need to find and kill endermen to harvest ender pearls for trading and creating a portal to the End. Endermen have been made tougher in various updates, and are now very tricky. They're difficult to hit with ranged attacks and have a lot of health. If you're going to take one on, ensure you're armoured, have a good, preferably enchanted diamond sword, and enlist the help of wolves. Building safe hidey holes can also help.

Endermen will stop attacking if they take damage from water or fire, and the arrival of daytime will usually make them teleport. Carrying a bucket of water to dump on them is always a good idea.

Endermen, although not purposely, can breach your defences by moving blocks and allowing animals or hostile mobs to jump over fences. So, if you hear or see one around, keep this in mind. Luckily, endermen can't move all blocks. Here's a list of blocks they can pick up and move: ● Cactus ● Clay ● Dirt ● Flowers ● Grass block ● Gravel ● Melon ● Mushrooms ● Mycelium ● Pumpkin ● Sand ● TNT

Wolves: Wolves can be found in the Overworld and will ignore you unless attacked. If provoked, the attacked wolf, and any other in the pack, will become hostile.

Once tamed, wolves (which become dogs) can follow the player, attacking anything that hurts their master, and they can be told to sit by using them. They can be fed to regain their health (signified by the angle of their tail), and you can breed them. They'll also teleport back to the player if they're too far away and not sitting.

Zombie Pigmen: Zombie pigmen are hybrids of pigs and zombies that wield swords. They're found primarily in the Nether, but can spawn near Nether portals (PC only). If attacked, the injured zombie pigman and all others in the immediate vicinity (32-block radius) will become hostile and attack the player. If killed, zombie pigmen will usually drop rotting flesh and gold nuggets, and may rarely drop gold ingots and gold swords. Picking them off one by one, isolating them from a pack, is the best tactic to use, and if pigmen don't see another attacked, they won't retaliate. Soul sand can slow them down, making them easier to fight and retreat from, and encasing yourself in a cobblestone booth can make things easier once a group is agitated. Don't underestimate zombie pigmen. They hit hard: a group of them can quickly overwhelm the unprepared player.

HOSTILE MOBS

Hostile mobs don't like you and they'll do all they can to take you down. If you find one, trouble is coming!

Blaze: Blazes are dangerous fire creatures found in the Nether. They can fly and will hurl fireballs at you, which damage you over time as you burn. Avoiding them may seem like the prudent action, but you'll need to kill these foes to harvest blaze rods. They can spawn normally in Nether fortresses and from spawn blocks, which make them even deadlier due to weight of numbers.

Tackling them requires careful planning and tactics, with the best approach being the use of fire resistance potions. When you first find them, however, you won't be able to brew these potions (you need a blaze rod to make a potion stand), so good armour and even a golden apple or two can help. Blazes can be damaged with any weapon, but ranged attacks with arrows are more preferable. They're also very vulnerable to snowballs, so bring your mittens.

Cave Spiders / Spiders: One of the most common hostile mobs is the spider. The normal variety is found all around the Overworld, and they're able to climb any structure, including fences.

Spiders are the best source of string (their webbing), which is an essential material, and they're relatively easy to kill most of the time. They're only hostile in low light levels, making them fairly harmless during the day. They also drop spider eyes, which are used in brewing.

Be careful if you encounter a spider in an abandoned mineshaft: it might be a cave spider. These behave just like normal spiders, but are stronger and able to poison you. This poison won't kill you on its own, but will drop your health to half a heart, making you easy pickings. Armour is no protection against poison.

Cave spiders are smaller than normal spiders and have a blue tint, can fit through smaller gaps, and they only spawn from monster spawners. Bright light can pacify them, so bring torches. The only way to stem the tide is to destroy the spawner they're coming from. Milk can be used to cure poison, so it's a good idea to have a couple of buckets on hand when exploring a mineshaft.

Creepers: The most instantly recognisable mob is the creeper. This silent foe is a dangerous suicide bomber that delights in sneaking up on unaware players before exploding. This explosion not only seriously damages (or kills) the player, but also the surrounding area. This can include your own structures, and can harm or kill tamed creatures. Creepers are arguably the most feared of non-boss mobs due to their knack for surprising players. Often, by the time you hear that dreaded hissing fuse, it's usually too late to react. Should you kill creepers though, they'll drop gunpowder, which is the easiest way to acquire it.

Creepers are one of the best pathfinders of all mobs, and can navigate complex environments to get to their targets. Due to their attack style, they're best dealt with by using ranged weapons like the bow. A sword can be

A zombie pigman

used, but you should carefully edge towards them, hit them once and back away before they blow. Repeat the process until they die. If you'd rather not tangle with a creeper, run 16 or more blocks away and they'll give up the chase. Eventually, creepers will despawn, so even if they're right outside your house you can usually wait them out, or sleep. Having cats around will scare creepers away.

There are a couple of special features you should know about creepers. They can be transformed into charged creepers if lighting strikes within 3-4 blocks of them. This makes them glow blue, and if they explode they do so with around 3-4 times the force of a normal creeper. They have less health and the same fuse time, but extra care should be taken.

Also, creepers are the only mobs that can drop music discs. To make this occur, you need to ensure that they're killed by a skeleton's arrow. You can damage the creeper beforehand (and this is the best way to ensure you get a disc), but the final blow must be dealt by a skeleton. Simply manoeuvre the creeper in between you and a skeleton, and if the arrow hits the creeper you'll get a disc.

Ghasts: Ghasts are found within the Nether and are huge, cube-shaped creatures that fly around hurling explosive fireballs. They emit chilling, infant-like noises, and can detect the player from a great distance (100 blocks). Often, you'll only know a ghast is around when a fireball explodes near you. They're immune to fire and water. If killed, they drop gunpowder and ghast tears, which are very valuable and quite rare. Ghast fireballs not only damage the player and the environment, but will also set fire to blocks. As much of the Nether is made of Netherrack, which burns forever if set alight, this can make for a very dangerous situation.

The easiest, and safest way to kill a ghast is to use 1-3 arrows (enchanted arrows may one-shot them). Lead your shots ahead of the ghast to account for its movement. Ghasts can also be killed using swords, but this is dangerous as you have to be close. You can also kill a ghast with its own fireball by hitting back at it with a melee attack or shooting it with an arrow. It's tricky, though. If you need shelter from ghast fireballs, the cheapest and most abundant block that resists their

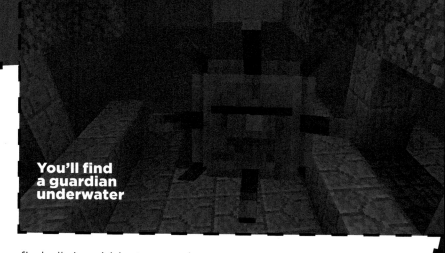

You'll find a guardian underwater

fireballs is cobblestone, so have some on you so you can build a barrier if needed.

Guardians and Elder Guardians: The first aquatic mobs in the game are the dangerous one-eyed guardians. These are found in and around ocean monuments. They can attack with spikes and a powerful, charged laser, which takes time to charge and deal damage. Elder guardians are far larger than normal, and their attacks can cause mining fatigue, which causes you to break blocks more slowly. Fighting guardians is tricky, as you'll be underwater. Arrows travel too slowly, so your sword is best. Be careful to avoid their lasers, and use a preferably diamond and enchanted sword. They drop prismarine crystals and shards, as well as raw fish. Elder guardians can also drop wet sponge, clownfish, raw salmon, or pufferfish.

Magma Cube: Similar to the Overworld's slimes, the Nether's magma cubes are bouncing blocks that can split into smaller creatures when hit and are immune to fire. When killed, they drop magma cream, which is used to make fire resistance potions. They can take a beating though, especially in larger forms, so caution is paramount. A good tactic to take them out is to shrink them down with an arrow or two, then wade in to finish the smaller cubes with your sword. Killing them also nets experience.

Silverfish: These small bugs are found hiding within monster eggs, usually found in strongholds, but sometimes in extreme hills biomes. If the monster eggs are mined, silverfish will swarm out and attack the player. They drop nothing when killed and yield little experience.

Monster eggs look like normal blocks (stone, cobblestone and stone brick), which take longer than usual to mine with a pickaxe, and less time without. If left alive, silverfish can hide within other blocks. They're easy enough to kill, but they can alert nearby silverfish, causing more problems. Single-hit kills with enchanted diamond swords work, as does dousing lava or dropping gravel.

Skeletons: One of the most annoying and equally effective mobs in the game. Skeletons are bow and arrow-wielding undead that can make your life a misery.

They can be very accurate with their arrows. As they can attack at range, even fences and other barriers prove useless. They're not too smart and will stupidly fire away at solid walls, and they burst into flames when caught in sunlight (unless in water or shade). When killed, they tend to drop arrows and bones, and sometimes drop bows and armour. Skeletons can pick up other weapons, but this is rare. They're easily detected thanks to their distinctive rattling noise.

Skeletons can be killed easily with arrows or melee weapons, and can often be fooled into attacking other mobs, such as endermen, zombies and other skeletons.

Slimes: Slimes are green, bouncing blocks of, er... slime. They can be found in varying sizes, and split into smaller slimes when attacked. They drop slimeballs when killed. Slimes are usually found deep underground, or in swamp biomes. Slimes deal more damage the bigger they are, so it's important to whittle them down from a distance first using arrows. When they're smaller, they can be killed easily enough with a sword.

Spider Jockeys: Two common foes – spiders and skeletons – unite here. They're able to attack at a distance and climb over any barrier. Luckily, spider jockeys are very rare, with around a 5% chance of one appearing when a spider spawns into the world. Killing the spider will leave the skeleton and, likewise, killing the skeleton will leave a miffed spider. The skeleton will also still burn in sunlight. Taking on a spider jockey is very dangerous due to the two-for-one attacks, but the rewards of bones, arrows, bows, string and spider eyes can be tempting. It's best to fight them if you have cover and a ranged weapon, otherwise they can kill quickly. Waiting until daytime so the skeleton is killed is one option, then you simply need to mop up the spider.

Witches: Witches look like villager mobs, but they're unfriendly and certainly won't trade with you. Along with skeletons, they're a ranged mob and live in witches huts in the Overworld. They attack using splash potions that can cause a number of effects, including poison,

slowness and weakness. They're almost immune to splash potions themselves. This makes them quite tricky to take on with anything other than a bow and arrow. Witches can drop glass bottles, glowstone dust, gunpowder, redstone, spider eyes, sticks and sugar in varying quantities. Rarely, they may also drop potions, including healing, fire resistance and swiftness.

Wither Skeletons: The Nether's version of skeletons are found in Nether fortresses. These darker-coloured undead wield stone swords and can not only inflict high damage, but also the wither status effect. This causes more damage for around ten seconds and can kill you. They're immune to fire and move faster than most mobs. If they find their way into the Overworld (through a portal), they're immune to sunlight. When killed, they drop bones and coal, and rarely wither skeleton skulls and stone swords.

Although they're tough, you can kill wither skeletons using the same basic attacking and backing off tactics used to take out creepers and zombies. Carefully edge towards them to get in a hit, then back away. Rinse and repeat. If you get hit, back off, let the wither status fade and go back in when you're healed. If you want to do battle with the wither boss then you'll need to kill enough wither skeletons to gather three skulls.

Zombies / Zombie Villagers

Zombies are both plentiful and bereft of brainpower, but they can still cause grief. They are slow-moving foes that converge upon players to do melee damage. They're vulnerable to sunlight and all weapons. They drop rotten flesh, carrots, potatoes and iron ingots and, in rare instances, drop shovels, swords and armour.

Zombies can appear in normal, baby, armed and villager guises. Babies are weaker and faster than normal, and armed zombies can use armour and

Along came a spider...

weapons. Villager zombies can spawn naturally, or as the result of a villager falling foul of zombie attack, and they can be cured using splash potions of weakness or by giving a golden apple.

Normal zombie attacks, if not in the form of an ambush, are easily dealt with, and attacking, backing off then attacking again is a good approach. Note that zombies can break through wooden doors on harder difficulties, meaning your home may not be as secure as you think unless you upgrade to iron doors. Like skeletons, zombies burn in direct sunlight and so die off in the morning.

A zombie

UTILITY MOBS

Utility mobs can be created by the player and fill the role of guardians. They're useful for defence, and can be created at any time.

Snow Golem: Snow golems are created using two stacked snow blocks with a pumpkin on top. Once created, they'll patrol the area, attempting to defend you from hostile mobs by throwing snowballs. They leave snow tiles in their wake, except in certain biomes, such as desert. Snow golems can be a useful distraction but, unless created in groups, are fairly useless. As they're made of snow, these utility mobs take melting damage in hot biomes like deserts and jungles, as well as contact with water. A good use for snow golems is for endermen defence: their snowball attack will make an enderman teleport away.

Iron Golem: Iron golems are created by making a T-shape out of four iron blocks, with a pumpkin for a head placed top-centre, making a cross (this must be placed last). Once created, iron golems will attack enemy mobs, but will always favour villager defence, as they're loyal to villager mobs. They also spawn naturally into the world in villages large enough to spawn them (at least 21 houses and ten villagers).

They have the highest hit points of any mob, except the ender dragon and wither, and can deal a lot of damage. Although slow, they're formidable warriors.

They suffer no fall damage and can't drown. Although they don't regenerate health, they're healed with splash health potions. If you build your own iron golem, you'll need to fence it in, as it will wander off. The only places they stay voluntarily are villages. They may even give flowers to villagers, such is their loyalty. Iron golems attack players who provoke them, but won't usually pursue unless villagers are attacked.

To keep control of an iron golem when wandering around, use a leash. This will force the golem to follow you, making it into a tough bodyguard to keep you safe whilst exploring. You can even tie them to fences.

BOSS MOBS

Finally: the two big ones to beat...

Ender Dragon: The first major boss is the ender dragon. It lives in the End, an alternate world that's also home to the endermen. To get to it you'll need to create and step through an End portal.

The ender dragon flies around the End, and will deal damage to the player with powerful projectiles and by coming into contact with them. It's healed by beacons found atop obsidian pillars strewn around the landscape. When killed, the ender dragon will drop an Overworld portal and a dragon egg. It will also yield a huge amount of XP (around 12,000).

The Wither: Unlike the ender dragon, the wither is an optional boss, and the player needs to build it themselves. It's arguably the most dangerous mob in the game. It's not only very powerful and can fly, but it can also rampage through the Overworld, attacking anything that moves. When active, the wither's three heads fire wither skulls, each of which does great damage and can inflict the wither status effect. When killed, the wither drops a Nether star, but only grants a measly 50 XP for all your effort.

MINECRAFT:

This is where we really start getting into the fun stuff! Once you've got settled into Minecraft, and wrapped your head around the basics, you can begin to get just a little more adventurous. Basically, it's time to get our hands dirty!

Thus, what we're going to look at in this chapter of the guide are some of the more advanced tips, tricks and strategies that can help you on your way to becoming a fully fledged expert!

As you can probably already see from the listing over on the right, we've got a lot to get through in this chapter. We're going to be looking in more detail at some of the foundation skills you need to really make the most of

Minecraft. After all, you're not going to get too far in the game if you struggle to simply stay alive! But then, we're also going to be dealing with the likes of trading, fishing, temples and farming. Even before that, we're going to be explaining how to furnish your home as you want it, then how to defend it from unwanted attacks!

This is the chapter where we get under the bonnet and look at the things you need to be on top of to get the most out of your time with Minecraft. Fortunately, it's the fun stuff too!

INTERMEDIATE

34-37	**NEVER DIG UP**
38-41	**STAYING ALIVE**
42-47	**FURNISHING YOUR HOME**
48-51	**DEFENDING YOUR HOME**
52-57	**FARMING**
58-59	**ANIMAL TAMING**
60-63	**COOKBOOK**
64-65	**BIOMES GUIDE**
66-67	**MINECARTS**
68-71	**NPC VILLAGES**
72-75	**VILLAGER TRADING**
76-77	**SWORDPLAY**
78-79	**GONE FISHIN'**
80-81	**TEMPLES**

NEVER DIG UP - MINING STRATEGIES

Searching for rare minerals and resources isn't just a necessity in Minecraft – it's probably the best part! There's something therapeutic about heading out into the world with nothing but your pickaxe and wits to survive on. Especially if you're playing in Peaceful mode, you can spend hours below ground just trying to hit that single cache of diamonds that'll provide you with the long-lasting tools you'll need for your next below-ground expedition!

But there's an art to creating a good mine – techniques that you'd probably learn through your own trial and error, which are helpfully described here. Follow these simple strategies and you'll find yourself mining like a pro.

NEVER DIG UP!

Perhaps the most basic tenet of Minecraft strategy. So basic, in fact, that game creator Notch felt the need to include it in the rotating messages on the game's title screen!

The logic is this: if you're in unfamiliar territory, you've got no idea what there might be two blocks above you. If you destroy the block directly between you and it, whatever's there could come bursting through. At best, it's nothing. At worst, it's gravel or sand that'll instantly crush you, or lava that'll fill your mineshaft with destructive lava, or water that'll sweep you over a nearby drop. Potential perils are everywhere!

The only circumstances in which you should destroy the block above you are those in which you know it's safe. If you're close enough to the surface that there's only dirt above you, you're probably okay – surface lava is acceptably rare, and gravel tends to rest above stone, not dirt.

If you must dig your way out of an unfamiliar hole, you can slowly work your way towards the surface by creating a makeshift staircase. But that's a strategy all on its own...

NEVER DIG DOWN!

If you're on a search for diamond and gold, you'll need to get yourself into the lower strata of the world. The quickest way to do this is to simply stand in one place and dig directly down. It's an attractive strategy if you're unable to find a sufficiently deep cave system. It's also a very easy way to get yourself killed – more so even than digging upwards!

The thing is, if you dig above yourself there's a chance you can move out of the way, or place a block in time to stop whatever horror you've unleashed from ending your life. When you're digging down, by the time you've spotted the lava or acknowledged that there's a long drop beneath you, it's already too late. There are no parachutes in Minecraft.

Falling into lava is a particularly grim manner of death – not just because of how quickly it takes hold, but because of the way it

Digging right down could drop you to your death in caves like this

incinerates everything you were carrying as well! You can potentially waste hours of work by dropping into molten rock. Digging down might be fast, but the risks aren't worth it.

Again, the exception to this rule is when you know what's beneath you. Building a tower beneath yourself and then mining it away is one of the quickest ways to get to and from high places, and a good way of avoiding drops that would otherwise kill you. Just don't be too reckless and you'll live to dig in any direction you like.

SIMPLE STAIRCASES

If you must dig your way up or down – perhaps because you're lost in a cave and need to reach the surface, or because you just can't find a cavern that goes down far enough – then a simple staircase makes much more sense than digging directly up or down. Admittedly, it's three times as much work because you have to dig out three blocks for every level you go up or down, but it's worth it for the safety you gain.

To dig a simple staircase, you

Lava is one of the most dangerous obstacles to find, not only hurting or killing you, but also destroying your items

must excavate the blocks directly in front of you. To move towards the surface, destroy the block in front of you and the two above it. To move down, destroy the block in front of you and the two below it. Digging upwards is still potentially perilous, but only if you encounter water or lava. To minimise the problems they cause, watch for droplets seeping through, which indicate the presence of water or lava so that you're prepared for what'll happen next. Keep stone or dirt adjacent to your pickaxe in the active inventory so that you can quickly plug any openings that reveal lava or water.

Digging down in this manner means you shouldn't encounter any serious problems, but take care when digging upwards into unfamiliar territory. You might be beneath the sea! As well as potentially flooding your cavern, particularly deep seas might cause you to drown before you reach the surface. If you can bring a map, they're a great help – maps will show you what's on the surface even if you're underground, minimising your chance of breaking through the sea bed!

A simple staircase. The only way to safely dig up or down

Simple staircases aren't the same as actual stairs – for a start, you have to jump up them – but in terms of getting up and down quickly they're simple, easy and safe.

THE MOST EFFICIENT MINING TECHNIQUE

This is where things get serious. Forget exploration, forget pioneering, forget anything except getting your hands on those cold, hard precious metals and gemstones. This is where mining stops being fun and starts being work. The most efficient mining practices can be a little tedious, but their brutal simplicity makes them both safe and likely to deliver results. If you want to guarantee diamonds, this is the way to do it.

To begin with, load up on pickaxes and then tunnel down to the very bottom of the world. You'll know you're there when you hit bedrock, the black and grey stripy blocks that are indestructible. You want to start digging a level or two above bedrock, to maximise your chance of finding ore and gems. If you tunnel AT bedrock level, 25-30% of blocks beneath you are guaranteed to be useless, which is inefficient!

Next, tunnel in a single direction for as long as you're happy to. You only need to create a 1x2 block passage big enough to fit through. Mine any useful blocks you encounter, and remember to keep it well lit. When you can't go any further (or think you've gone far enough), stop. This is now the main shaft for your mine. Now return to the start and begin mining a new passage perpendicular to the main one. Again, go for as long as you like, collecting blocks along the way. When you're done, turn and begin mining a passage parallel to the main one. You only need to carve three blocks forward, so that there's a gap of two blocks between the passage you just carved and the one you're about to create. Mine until you return to the main shaft, move another three blocks over, and start the process again.

This technique, grimly mechanical though it is, will help you scope out the greatest number of blocks for the least amount of effort. Each section of passage you mine will show you at least six new blocks. Creating passages two blocks apart means you won't see blocks twice, nor will you miss any. Admittedly, you'll end up creating a maze of uninteresting passages, but the incidence of diamond is such that if you find enough to make one diamond pick, you should find enough to make at least two before that one runs out. The rewards are worth it!

USE LAVA AND WATER TO YOUR ADVANTAGE

The way lava and water blocks are generated means that if you encounter them underground, they're almost always attached to a wider cavern network. Caverns, being essentially

pre-excavated, have a lot of exposed blocks and are therefore great places to look for rare minerals and ores without having to do a lot of mining.

That means if you're carving out a passage in stone and you hit lava or water, you shouldn't just stop and turn around. Plug the gap and 'feel' your way around the edges. If you've got glass blocks available, they're a good way of letting you create a map of where the lava or water is flowing to/from. Your goal should be to get up high and find the source of the flow you've encountered. Nine times out of ten you'll be led to a cave system teeming with easily accessible coal and iron, and lower down there's a very good chance of finding gold and diamond too.

DON'T GET LOST

A particularly protracted bout of exploration is fun, but the further you go, the easier it is to get lost. Compasses and maps won't help if you're stuck at the end of a labyrinthine cave system with no tools and no idea how to get back, after all, and retracing your steps only works if you can recognise one cave fork from another. Hardly simple.

The best thing to do is find a system that'll help you orient yourself. You could block off passages once you've explored them to minimise the chance you'll take a wrong turn more than once. You could pick up torches as you pass them so that you know there's no point heading twards darker caves. You could even leave a trail of redstone back to the entrance as you venture into the cave, but only if you're extra organised.

The important thing is not to rely on your memory alone. You might think you know what you're doing, but spend too long underground and you'll soon lose track of how to get out. Carving your way back to the surface with your bare hands might be preferable to a voluntary suicide, but a little forward planning and you'll be able to get out with all of your resources (and nerves) intact!

STAYING ALIVE: 9 SURVIVAL TIPS

Dying in Minecraft is no big deal early on – you just wake up at the spawn point and get back to work replacing the paltry quantities of wood, coal, dirt and stone you were carrying. No harm done.

However, once you've been playing a few hours, or even a few days, dying can become a real drag. Sure, you'll reappear at home, safe and secure in your well-defended bed, but your inventory will take a lot more work to replace. It can set you back untold amounts of time. Maybe even sap your will to continue.

There's only one way you can avoid this grim fate: you've got to stay alive. And that means keeping your wits about you: knowing how to reduce the odds of death with a sharp mind and keen senses. Or, at best, learning how to spot deadly situations before you blunder straight into them. If you think Ray Mears and Bear Grylls have it tough, wait until you've spent a night alone in the world of Minecraft...

TIP 1:
ALWAYS CARRY SPARE FOOD

Assuming you're not playing on Peaceful mode (in which case surviving isn't difficult), there are only three ways to replenish health in Minecraft: drinking potions, keeping your hunger bar full, or standing on a beacon. Potions and beacons are difficult to obtain for much of the game (there's a reason we've placed both of those in the Advanced section), so your only alternative is to stock up on food. The general rule is to keep enough food on you to replenish your entire hunger bar at least twice. Cooked steak and porkchops both replenish 8 points and are easy to obtain early on. Try not to eat unless you've actively taken damage, because a full hunger bar is of no practical value if you're not injured.

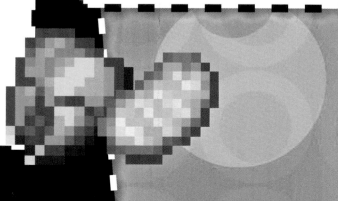

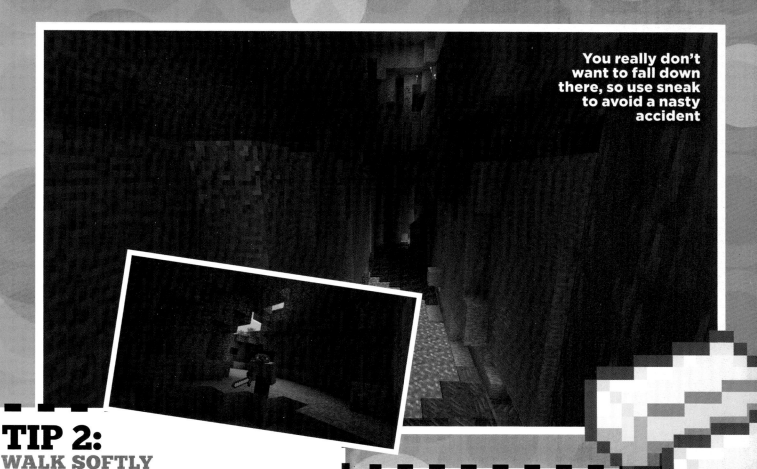

You really don't want to fall down there, so use sneak to avoid a nasty accident

TIP 2:
WALK SOFTLY

Whether you're shimmying along a ravine, scaling a cliff face, climbing a tree or edging past a lava pit, you can never overuse the sneak mode. Sneaking is accessed on the PC version by holding down Shift while you move, or on the console by pressing the right analogue stick, and will cause you to crouch slightly and move considerably slower than a regular walk. But more interestingly for your survival chances, you can't fall while in sneak mode, greatly reducing the chance of you slipping to your death.

There are other benefits too – sneaking allows you to build outcrops and bridges, because it's possible to place a block on the ledge beneath you without falling, and it will hide your nametag from anyone more than five blocks away in multiplayer. But a guarantee you won't plunge to your death is undoubtedly its most useful effect.

TIP 3:
DON'T GET GREEDY

This is one of those tips that probably won't really sink in until you've made the mistake for yourself, but take it from those who know: it's better to come back with a little treasure than lose it all because you wanted to know what riches might be around that next corner. Know when to call it a day and turn back.

And when might that be? Well, whenever you've got what you came for is a good time to stop. Or whenever you start to feel lucky to have found so much. That's the time to get back to your base and deposit the rewards you've collected. The longer you're away from home, the more your resources dwindle, the easier it is to die and the greater the losses for actually dying. Try not to make that mistake, even though you inevitably will.

A measured and cautious approach to mining can yield bountiful results

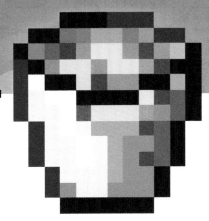

TIP 4:
USE LAVA AS A WEAPON

You don't have to play Minecraft for long to know that lava will bring about a swift end to even the most experienced player, but did you know it's good for offing your enemies too? A bucket of lava can be one of the game's most powerful offensive weapons, as long as you know how to use it.

All you need to do is obey two simple rules: Stand Back and Get Up High. Especially in enclosed spaces, lava can quickly wipe out multiple enemies and it doesn't lose durability when you use it. Admittedly, it's as likely to kill you, and it will incinerate anything your enemies drop, but it beats engaging in swordplay. Remember: the best fights are the ones you don't even have to start.

TIP 5:
FOLLOW A GOOD MINING STRATEGY

If you're trying not to die, it's important to remember the cardinal rules and follow them at all times: never dig directly up, and never dig directly down. The secret to staying alive is to never assume anything and treat every action like it's about to place you in mortal danger. Eventually, you'll recognise the value of standing back while digging up or down – probably on the day the floor beneath you opens up onto a ravine, or the ceiling caves in to reveal a cascade of gravel that would have smashed you flat. A careful player is a long-lived one.

TIP 6:
CLOCK AND COMPASS

Like Phileas Fogg, any Minecraftian explorer will soon learn the value of proper timekeeping and orienteering. Maps are useful, but only as long as you're within their boundaries. Eventually, you'll travel off the edge, at which point they become nothing but some intricately decorated bits of paper. Carry a compass with you at all times and you'll be able to keep track of whether you're heading to or from your most recent spawn point.

Similarly, a clock will help you know whether it's safe to go above ground when you're off spelunking, and give you an always visible reminder of how close it is to getting dark. Staying informed and prepared will keep you alive longer than simply reacting will!

TIP 7:
ARMOUR UP!

Wearing a full complement of iron armour is a great way to stay alive. Not only does it reduces the damage you take during mob attacks, it also reduces damage from other sources like explosions, fire, lava and cacti. It takes a little work before you'll have enough iron ingots to create your first full set of armour, but after you've been playing for a while you'll have more iron than you'll ever realistically need. Top it up when you can and don't worry if you end up with loads of half-broken equipment - you can always use an anvil to combine old parts into something more durable!

Sir Steve dons his iron armour ready for another journey

TIP 9:
ORGANISE YOUR INVENTORY HOTBAR

Staying alive means reducing the amount of time between thinking and acting, and that means making sure your hotbar – the section of 'active' inventory visible at the bottom of the screen – is tailored to your exact needs.

You'll find your own preferred configuration in time, but, ideally, you should have torches, a weapon, a spade, a pick, some spare blocks (for quickly sealing gaps or building steps), a bucket and compass available. Keep the layout the same, and soon you'll be able to go from defense to offense without thinking. That kind of speed can save your life!

TIP 8:
TAKE WOOD UNDERGROUND

You can find almost anything underground – metals, stone, minerals, water and lava are all in abundant supply – but it's incredibly rare to find wood, unless you chance upon a disused minecart track or dungeon. Even then, it's likely to be surrounded by mobs.

Wood is vital for crafting torches, signs, fences, furniture, tools, chests and crafting tables, and even though there's almost none underground, you can barely move for it up top! If you've got it going spare, why not take a set of 64 unprocessed logs with you below ground? You can never have too much wood!

There's no shortage of wood on the surface, so don't forget to take some underground with you

When the Minecraft world seems all too unrelenting, and you just can't stand being blown up, skewered, stung, beaten or eaten any more, the best place to retreat to has to be home. When nights are long, you need a way to pass the time, whether the aim of your game be to create big elaborate works of art or simply get to the End and show that dragon who's boss, making your house a little more inviting can be just as useful as it is fun.

Why not make your Minecraft house a home while you wait for the sun to banish your enemies with this fabulous furnishing guide?

FURNISHING

SETTING UP SHOP

Firstly, you'll need a house, whether modest or a massive stone fortress. Once you have one, you can begin setting up the basics you need. But you'll soon discover all kinds of material that can tickle your creative fancy, right on your doorstep and beyond. We're going to look at all the different furnishings you can make to go in your home. Note that not all things are functional. Some are purely for decoration. That said, decoration can make a space seem much more impactful and interesting.

THE KITCHEN

This is a great room in which to keep your crafting table, your furnace and your food chests. If you've constructed your house or room with double-block walls, you can place all three of these items in the walls to save space. Note that in order for a storage chest to open, it must have a block of empty space above it, allowing the lid to be lifted. This allows the possibility of placing a chest in the floor or in a wall given that there's nothing placed on top of it. Crafting tables and furnaces don't need this extra space and you can place one on top of the other. You can also construct sinks of water, tables, chairs, refrigerators, and all kinds of kitchen furniture.

Tables and chairs can be created in many ways. The simplest is to place a single fence post with a pressure plate on top. They can be lined up next to each other to make longer tables. Chairs are

Set useful blocks like crafting tables and furnaces into the wall to save space

If you want your sink to be functional, you're going to need to make a well.

A well provides an infinite supply of water and won't dry up, but is much larger. Start by making a 4x4 block square, be it against a wall or wherever you prefer. To save space, you can build your sink half in and half out of a wall, as long as you can reach the water once it

YOUR HOME

It's easy to create a simple table and chair set

simply stairs placed around a table. Make armchairs by placing signs on either side.

Sinks can also be made in different ways. You can make one by digging one block and filling it with water, which would need to be refilled should you use it. You can also use a cauldron, which holds only three bottles worth of water and would also need to be refilled. These sinks are best created as decoration only.

has been placed. When you've made your square, which only needs to be one block high, build the edge of the sink with your chosen material, then use two buckets of water to evenly fill the 2x2 block space in the middle (use a bucket on each diagonally adjacent corner). This will create still water and allow you to refill your buckets whenever you need to in the comfort of your own kitchen. If you want to make it look realistic, you

You can create a simple sink with infinite water

can use a tripwire hook as a tap as well, although this wouldn't function and would be solely decorative.

Refrigerators can be made in a number of ways. The easiest is simply placing two blocks of quartz, iron or snow on top of each other; however, this isn't a functional refrigerator. For it to be functional, you'll need a chest, a block of snow, iron or quartz, an iron door and a lever. Choose the place you want your fridge to be. This is usually best in a wall, three blocks high with blocks either side. Remove one lowest, floor-level block, in which you'll place your chest, and don't place anything in the block directly above it or your chest won't open. Above this empty block, place your snow, iron or quartz. Now to place your door, which can be tricky. You won't be able to place it against the space in which you've placed your chest, as technically it doesn't have a floor block. Instead, place it in front but to the side of the nook you've made in the wall. Place the lever next to it so that when you pull the lever the door closes and covers the chest and snow block. One fridge.

Cupboards aren't functional but can make a kitchen look genuine. Simply place a bookshelf and on it a trapdoor. Close the trapdoor and it will resemble a cupboard with colourful food items.

A living room is more about fun than function

LIVING ROOM

A living room is usually a place to invite your friends to spend time in when they visit, or maybe to watch telly. In the game, this may seem obsolete as these things can't be done and a lot of the things occupying a living room may not be functional. But this room adds to the escapist's idea of realism, providing you with visual flights of fancy to lighten up your home.

Sofas can be made in the same way as chairs with stair blocks, but by placing several next to each other. You can make this look more authentic using different materials. You can also use the signpost arm trick, and alternatively use wooden slabs and signs to make a different style of sofa.

It's possible to make a realistic-looking kitchen with a little effort

Fireplaces are a great focal point for any living room, and add a little warmth to the pixels that surround us. In Minecraft, a fireplace is achievable using Netherrack and lava. You can simply knock a few blocks out of your wall, or you can create a large ornate fireplace with a chimney.

A simple, but effective armchair

Either way, you need to leave some space at the bottom of your chimney to place your Netherrack blocks and, when you're ready, simply light them using flint and steel. If using lava, be sure to contain it well, as if it spills the damage is often fierce. Regardless of which source of heat you choose, it's important to surround your fireplace with non-flammable materials, so it may be an idea to hold that carpet and go for a protective stone hearth.

Most living rooms have ornaments and decorations, and Minecraft's versions needn't be any different. Paintings are an easy way to decorate the living room (and any other area of the house), and by placing them on the wall over and over, you can cycle through the random artwork to find one you like. If there's enough space, you can also use larger or longer-sized paintings.

Item frames can be crafted and can hold items placed into them, and are very versatile. Not only can they be used to simply show off your items, but you can place working clocks and compasses in them, and even maps will function. You can rotate items placed in them, and by using combinations of blocks and tools, you can craft some nice modern art for your in-game living room.

You can create some grandiose fireplaces, complete with potted plants and hunting trophies

Another good addition to the living room is the new armour stand. This decorative item can be used to show off your finely crafted armour in all its protective glory. Armour stands are made with six sticks and a stone slab; once

Armour stands can show off your blacksmith skills

Clocks can be placed on the wall so you'll always know what time it is

crafted and placed, if you're using your armour elsewhere, you could place other stuff – like pumpkins and mob heads – on display instead.

BEDROOMS

One of the most functional rooms is the bedroom, as sleeping lets you jump to the next day. This makes it safer to wander around, and also stops some mobs spawning, and despawns others (this happens when players sleep).

For the bed, you can easily place two next to each other to make a double, and placing the beds in a one-block deep hole makes for an interesting sunken effect. You can even construct bunk beds. For one method, on a wall with a 4x4 area free, place fence posts along the left and right sides, then place wooden planks on the bottom layer between the fence posts. Place the bed on top of the block, then destroy the planks. Repeat above the bed to place the second.

Another design uses doors instead. Place two blocks next to each other, then place doors either side flush against the block. Now, place a bed on top of the two blocks and destroy the blocks, leaving only the bed. Place a bed where the blocks were and you're done.

Bunk beds are only really for decoration and not for sleep. It's worth noting, however, that you should test your beds before you use them. Always ensure

The are usually many ways to do everything in Minecraft

you can actually stand up on them before you sleep. If there's not enough room, and you go to sleep, when you wake you can be squashed by the ceiling and die.

For that last little touch, you can place single chests either side of the bed as side tables, and these double up as personal storage too. Bookshelves and lamps also have a nice effect.

So, where does a pixellated miner put his or her clothes? In a dresser, of course, and you can fashion them in various ways. The easiest way to create them is to simply stack two chests onto each other. Alternatively, you can use double-stacked wooden planks and place buttons, trap doors or even signposts on them, with zeros as the text to make the handles.

Of course, when you're not down the mines, you may want to check out Facebook and keep in touch with friends – but to do that, you need a computer. To make one, place a block for the computer table down, then place a block of coal on top. Put an item frame on the block of coal and inside place a filled map to make the monitor. Next, place another block to the side or in front of the monitor, and place an activator rail – this makes a good keyboard.

If you like music and want a piano,

simply place a jukebox and note block next to each other against a wall, then place two Nether brick stairs on top of them, facing towards you. You've now got yourself a simple note-playing piano that will also play music if you insert a disc.

LIGHTING

Household lights (and lights in other rooms) are easily made using redstone lamps, which look better than the usual coal torches. These can even be turned on and off using switches. For that extra special touch, though, you can make automatic lights that turn on at night and off during the day.

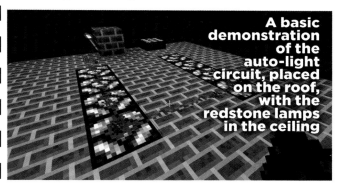

A basic demonstration of the auto-light circuit, placed on the roof, with the redstone lamps in the ceiling

To do this, all you need is a light sensor, redstone torch, one or more redstone lamps and redstone wire, plus a block of any type. Place the light sensor where it will catch the light (either outside, on the roof or inside if you have a skylight), then use wire to link the sensor to a block. Place the redstone torch on the opposite side (this turns it off if the sensor is powered, which in daylight it will be) then use more wire to link the torch to the redstone lamp(s).

This simple setup will now activate the light at night time and turn it off during the day. You can, of course, experiment with this configuration and place lamps in the ceiling or walls. Whichever works for you.

CAT FLAPS

If you've got cats, or even dogs, you'll know how annoying it can be having to open doors for them, or waiting for them to teleport after you. You can make things easier, though, by making a cat flap of sorts. To do this, simply knock a single-sized hole in an exterior wall then place a fence gate inside. On either side of the wall, place a pressure plate. That's it, you've now got a working cat flap, which can also be used by dogs, but is too small for hostile mobs.

A couple of pressure plates and a fence gate mean your pets can come and go as they please

DEFENDING YOUR HOME

You'll need to defend your new home from all sorts of attack. Here are some helpful tips to keep your base of operations safe

So, you've spent countless hours mining for materials to build your home. A lot of hard work later you have a truly impressive structure. Then, all of a sudden, boom! A creeper comes along and blows part of it up. Gah!

Thankfully, this situation can be avoided with a few simple steps.

LOCATION

Before you lay a block, your first task is to pick a good place to build your home. This should be a large enough area to build in and not crammed into the middle of a dense jungle. Being Minecraft, you can bend any area to your will with enough tools and time, but it's far easier and less time confusing if you pick a spot that's at least partly suitable to begin with.

It's not just space that's important, though; it's the actual location, and this is especially relevant when thinking about security. If you build your home in an area that's surrounded by trees or cliffs, you're effectively blinding yourself to enemy attack. At night, enemies can sneak right up unseen and, in the case of a creeper, that's not good.

Building next to tall structures can also make it easy for enemies to jump down onto your land, and trees can grow into your land, causing niggles when you're moving around or building.

For these reasons, you should always

Areas of dense forest and jungle aren't the best places to build

pick an area with clear visibility around it and as little in the way of tall structures nearby as possible. This gives you plentiful visibility and less chance of mobs using higher blocks to jump over fences and the like.

Flat spaces, like deserts are good, defensible locations

Also avoid building your home next to an NPC village. This may sound like a good idea at the time, and is certainly useful for easy trading and even ready-made buildings you can pinch, but at night, when the zombie horde comes calling, you'll wish you'd built it somewhere more remote, unless you fortify the village beforehand.

Having resources like wood, water and stone nearby is a definite bonus too, but, as we're talking about security here, visibility is key.

BASIC DEFENCES

Assuming you've got a nice home with a few crops and animals, your first step should be to protect it from mob attack.

The most basic and effective method of defence is to build fences, lots of fences. Although they appear to be only one block high, they do, in fact, have a 1.5 block height, meaning mobs can't jump over them (nor can you). Only spiders and spider jockeys can pass these, and endermen can teleport past them. If you're on a horse, you can also jump them.

So, surround your property with fencing, making sure you have plenty of space between the fence and your buildings and animals. Remember, a creeper can still explode if on the other side of a fence. In fact, an outer perimeter fence and an internal fence can be even more effective, offering a no-man's land buffer zone. Just don't forget to put some fence gates in or you'll be stuck. Wooden fence is the easiest to obtain, but can be set on fire or blown up easily. You can make stronger fencing out of Netherbrick. This

has twice the durability and can't be set on fire.

Always ensure you have as much light as you can around your property. Many mobs can only spawn in darker areas, so even if you fence off the area, mobs can still spawn inside your grounds if the lighting isn't bright enough. Place torches on the fences around your land, on your building exteriors, rooftops and in animal pens. If there are large, empty areas in your land, build towers with lamps on to blanket everywhere.

Fences should render the next step moot, but later, harder difficulties allow zombies to break through wooden doors. So, if you don't want to use fence for any reason, or you just want to be doubly protected, invest in some iron doors.

These can't be broken by zombies and are totally secure. However, they also can't be opened by hand. To open them, you need to place a switch, pressure pad or lever next to them, or use redstone circuits.

If you'd rather not use iron doors, you can always place wooden doors next to each other. This will delay zombies, giving you chance to kill them before they make it inside.

Tamed wolves are another

Wooden doors won't keep zombies at bay on Hard

great form of general defence, and when placed around your grounds can help defend your home. Golems are also very useful, especially iron golems, although you'll need to fence them in to stop them wandering. Be careful though, as they can also cause problems.

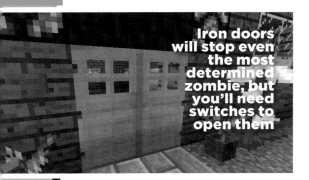
Iron doors will stop even the most determined zombie, but you'll need switches to open them

Snow golems, for example, like to leave trails of snow behind them, and open doors as they wander around, potentially making holes in your security.

PERIMETER DEFENCE

You may have fencing surrounding your home, and enough lighting to keep mobs from spawning inside, but at some point you still have to venture outside, so it's a good idea to protect the surrounding area too. There are a few techniques you can use to make things a little more secure.

As creepers are one of the most problematic foes, you may want to think about ways to control them.

A great prevention technique is to find and tame ocelots (which become cats). These are the only mob that a creeper is afraid of, and they'll run away from them. Place them around your property, and they should drive away any creepers. Sadly, ocelots aren't all that common, found only in jungle biomes, and they can be tricky to tame.

One of the most basic other approaches to take is to dig a load of holes three or more blocks deep in the ground in a chequerboard pattern. Although creepers will try to avoid drops, so many holes can often cause them to fall in and, once there, they can't escape.

In fact, you can easily trick creepers and other mobs into falling into pit traps. To do so, dig your pit then place signs on the inside lip of the pit. This sign is seen as a full, solid block by mobs, so they'll walk right into the pit.

If you dig another hole and place a cactus at the bottom (the holes will need to be at least 3x3, as you can't place cacti adjacent to other solid blocks, and then only on sand), you've got a simple death trap, as cactus blocks hurt mobs that touch them, as well as you.

If you're a bit of a pyromaniac, grab some Netherrack and use it as the base of the pit, then set it on fire with a flint and steel. You'll have a firetrap, effective against any enemies.

Another material from the Nether that's useful in defence is soul sand. This slows down anything that walks over it, and can make shooting creepers and skeletons much easier. If you place sections of soul sand around your land, it can be very useful. Another way to accomplish this is to spread cobwebs around, as mobs will also get caught up on these

Webs will slow s, including pers, making them er to deal with

(except spiders). You'll need to use shears to harvest cobwebs when you find them, or a sword enchanted with Silk Touch, otherwise webs will be picked up as string.

Thanks to redstone circuits, there's a huge array of devices you can create, many of which can be used for defence (see the Redstone Circuits section of the guide), and there are some contraptions you can use if you're no circuit expert.

One of the most effective is an arrow dispenser. If you create one, or a few if you want to cover more areas, you can link them, using redstone wire, to pressure pads. When the pad is pressed by a mob, an arrow will fire at them. Arrows are expensive, though, so you may want to make sure you farm those chickens.

BE VIGILANT

Most defences and traps are effective against almost all enemies, but there are a couple of foes that delight in bucking the trend. In the Overworld, these are mainly spiders, spider jockeys and the creepy endermen.

Spiders and spider jockeys can climb any structure and jump over any fences, rendering your efforts useless. Spiders aren't that worrying, and only attack at night most of the time, but spider jockeys are far more troublesome. If your combat skills aren't great, get indoors and wait for the skeleton to burn up in sunlight.

Endermen aren't a threat most of the time unless you provoke them. However, they can easily undermine your defences, as they can not only pinch blocks of certain types, but also place blocks next to your fences, thus allowing mobs to jump over. If you hear an enderman outside, be sure to check your perimeter, just in case.

If you take enough precautions, you shouldn't have any issues with creeper attacks, but it's worth noting that creeper explosions, like all others in the game, affect some blocks more drastically than others. So, if you build your house out of wood and dirt, expect a creeper attack to take a good portion of your home with it when it goes pop. Building out of stone or

This is a basic arrow dispenser trap. Stepping on the plate fires an arrow

brick, however, will give you substantially more protection. Materials like obsidian will make you virtually immune. So, build structures out of stone at the very least, and also use stronger materials as foundations, otherwise a blast may leave the house, but will still create a huge hole underneath.

FARMING

CROPS

Farming can be done with many items and creatures. It's a good idea to start with the farming of crops such as wheat, as it can come in very handy when farming animals. Wheat crops also produce bales of wheat for making foods such as bread, cakes and cookies.

Triangular ferns

Dead plants

Long grass

To start, you'll need a hoe, and some seeds. You can find seeds by destroying triangular ferns found in the jungle, dead-bush looking plants found in the desert or tall grass, which is the most common and grows in most areas excluding the desert. This can be done by hand, with blocks, with tools and even weapons, as you see fit. When you destroy a block of tall grass, it will occasionally drop seeds, but not always, so you may need to destroy quite a few before having enough to begin a crop. Once you get started, you can collect up to three seeds from one block of fully matured wheat every time you harvest it, along with one bale of wheat.

Tilled dirt using a hoe

When you've chosen where to begin planting seeds, select your hoe and use it whilst aimed at a dirt or grass block in order to till the dirt and create a block of farmed land. Once you've tilled the dirt and created farmed land, you should plant your seeds quickly, as farmed land can turn

Good irrigation will mean crops grow faster

A patch of seeds to grow wheat

back into dirt if it's then left unattended.

Once you have farmed land, it's important not to place anything on top of it either before or after you've planted seeds. Stepping on or placing other blocks on farmed land causes it to turn back into a dirt block, and any seeds planted will usually pop out, available to be collected and then replanted.

Fully grown wheat, ready for harvesting

In order to grow, crops need plenty of light. If not direct sunlight, it's important to surround your crops with torches. This allows you to grow crops under cover and at night. The more light, the quicker your crops will grow. Torches also prevent mobs from spawning in and around your crops. If mobs spawn or walk on them, your crops will be destroyed. For this reason, it can be a good idea to place fencing around your crops to prevent them being trampled.

Irrigated crops

When farming land, it's wise to have water nearby. Hydrated farmland allows crops to grow faster. That said, you can still grow crops without water; it simply takes longer. It takes five minutes to grow crops under ideal conditions, and up to 35 minutes under the worst conditions. You'll know when your wheat crops are fully grown as they develop little dark tips in their final stage of growth.

Potatoes, fully grown
Carrots, fully grown

Like wheat, you can grow a number of other things on a farmed block of land, including pumpkins, potatoes, melons and carrots. Potatoes and carrots must be planted directly into farmed land instead of harvesting seeds from them first. Melon and pumpkin seeds grow into a vine, which will then spawn melons and pumpkins on any adjacent empty dirt or grass

Pumpkins

blocks, so it's generally a good idea to allow them some extra room.

There are a number of other plants that can be farmed without using farmed land. These include sugar cane, cacti, vines, trees and cocoa beans.

Melons

Sugar cane farming can be achieved by selecting a piece of sugar cane, aiming at either a dirt, grass or sand block and selecting use. In order for sugar cane to grow, it needs to be planted on a block that

Allow room for growth

is placed directly next to water. The water can be either still or flowing as long as it's directly in contact with the block the sugar cane is planted on. Sugar cane can take quite a while to grow, and when harvesting it's best to harvest from the second block up from the ground, allowing the

Sugar cane
Harvested sugar cane

sugar cane to regrow without needing to be replanted.

Cactus is one of the more difficult crops to farm and can be achieved by placing a cactus block directly onto a block of sand. The sand you place it on should be elevated, with no other blocks next to the cactus or it won't grow. Beware when farming cactus plants, as it can prove quite dangerous. If you come in contact with the cactus plant, it will harm you. You can avoid this by placing a block directly above and to one side of the cactus. This will trim the new cactus as it grows. The next, more difficult step is to build a kind of moat in the ground below the sand in which your cactus is planted. Ensure the water is flowing to one or two points, where it will wash all the pieces of new cactus that drop, making them easier and safer to collect. The primary benefit of farming cactus is that it's used to make green dye and can also be used to protect your property. To learn more about using cactus in a defensive manner see Defending Your Home.

A crop of cacti

Vines are easier to grow and can initially be found in jungle and swamp biomes. In order to collect a vine you must use shears, otherwise you simply destroy the vine and are unable to collect it. Planting vines is relatively easy; you simply place the vine on the side of any solid block, including walls and ceilings. Once a vine is planted, it will grow slowly downward and across the structure on which it's planted, including across open spaces such as doorways or windows. Vines won't, however, grow within one block above a torch, and this can be a useful way to tame vines and keep them from spreading. Vines can be climbed much like a ladder, and you can look at endermen through vines without them attacking you.

Trees are relatively easy to farm. They can be planted on dirt or grass and don't require much special treatment. You plant trees as saplings, which are dropped when the leaves of a tree are destroyed or despawn. Simply select your sapling, aim at the block you wish to plant it on and select use – not unlike planting most other things. One thing to note is, depending on the type of tree you're planting, oak, spruce, birch or jungle tree, they'll grow to different sizes and require a certain amount of space between them in order to have enough sunlight to grow. All in all, the benefit of tree farming lies in the constant wood they provide. Oak trees will often provide apples as well, and all trees provide you with more saplings, allowing you to replant them.

Freshly planted birch trees

Cocoa bean farming can be useful, as cocoa beans are often tricky to come by. They can be planted on the side of any jungle wood blocks, be it a living tree or a harvested block, and don't require a specific level of light. When planting cocoa beans, select your beans, aim at the side of the wood block or tree and select use. A cocoa pod will then appear and, when matured, will produce up to three bunches of cocoa beans when destroyed. It's useful to note that if you leave spaces between each pod when you plant them, they'll grow faster than ones planted above, below or beside other pods.

Cocoa pods, fully grown

Collect the beans by destroying a pod

A very useful tip for growing many of the above crops is to use bonemeal (made from, what else? Bones). When applied to some crops and plants, bonemeal can instantly accelerate growth to a later stage or full maturity. However, it can take as many as ten helpings of bonemeal to achieve full growth.

Bonemeal

Bonemeal can be used on wheat, potatoes, carrots, melon and pumpkin vines, tree saplings, mushrooms (which will then grow into huge mushrooms), cocoa and grass (which can also produce flowers). It's no use when growing sugar cane, Nether Wart, cactus or vines.

One of the most important uses of wheat and seeds is that they can be used to lure and breed livestock and chickens. This leads us to our next level of farming – animals.

ANIMALS

Cows, chickens, pigs, sheep, and now rabbits are all very profitable animals in the Minecraft world.

Cows are the largest of the four, and provide leather, beef and milk. When a cow is killed, it drops up to two pieces of leather and up to three pieces of raw beef.

A group of chickens

The rarer form of cow, the mooshroom, can also be farmed. This can be difficult, though, as mooshrooms are found in mushroom biomes, which are usually islands surrounded by water. This means you may need to exercise some caution in luring your mooshroom to its enclosure. If you can manage this, mooshrooms are not only an infinite source of mushroom stew when you milk them with a wooden bowl, but they drop beef and leather, and you can milk them like any other cow using a bucket. This makes them an infinitely valuable source of many types of food. If you sheer a mooshroom, as you would a sheep, you gain five red mushrooms. However, this does turn them into normal cows, and takes away their ability to provide mushrooms and mushroom stew.

Chickens are the smallest farm animal and, when killed, provide raw chicken and feathers. When alive, chickens lay eggs and can breed. A single chicken will usually lay an egg every five to ten minutes or so. Be sure to collect your chicken eggs regularly, as they'll eventually despawn. In order to hatch an egg, select it, aim at the spot you want the chick to appear and select use. You'll throw the egg and it will either hatch a chick or smash. One in eight eggs will produce a chick, and about one in 32 eggs will produce four chicks instead of just one.

An egg that failed to hatch a chick

Eggs that hatch successfully produce chicks

Pigs provide up to three raw porkchops when killed, and can be saddled and ridden. (Check out our guide to Animal Taming to learn how to ride a pig.)

Rabbits are a more recent addition to the game and, although you may be loathed to do so, killing them gives you rabbit meat, as well as a possible rare drop of a rabbit's foot, used for potion making. They also drop rabbit hide. Be sure to keep them away from your carrot crops, though, as they'll eat them.

Sheep drop wool, used for many tasks, and also mutton. Alongside mutton, they'll drop one piece of wool when killed and up to three pieces when sheared. Aside from the advantage of gaining more wool when you spare their lives, not killing sheep means they'll regrow their fleece, allowing you to shear them over and over again. Sheep need to be kept in grassed areas, as they eat grass in order to regrow their wool.

Wool is a great commodity in the Minecraft world, and it can be used to make many things. If you want to add a little colour to your wool, it's possible to do so using

A shorn sheep

dye. However, to create more coloured wool using less dye, you can apply any coloured dye directly to a sheep with a full fleece, and any wool it drops and regrows after that point will remain that colour. Simply select the dye in a colour of your choice, aim at the sheep and select use. Wool can also be made without keeping sheep using the string you collect from killing spiders. However, this could prove slightly more hazardous, as spiders can harm you, and no-one likes spiders.

To learn how to make wool or dye, check out the Crafting Glossary.

BREEDING

All of these animals can be lured and bred. Cows (including mooshrooms) and sheep are lured using wheat. To lure, simply select the wheat so you're holding it in your hand and they'll follow you. This is especially useful when you're trying to lure them into an enclosure that you've established for them to live in.

In order to breed, instead of simply holding the wheat,

aim at the cow or sheep you wish to breed and select use. The wheat will disappear when used and the animal will enter into 'love mode'. You'll know this has worked when you see little red love hearts begin to float up from the animal's head. You then have a short time to do the same with another animal of the same species in order for them to breed. When they breed, it will appear as

Two cows breeding

Two cows and a calf

though the two animals are nuzzling each other. If you don't select another animal, love mode will eventually end and the animal will return to normal.

Pigs can only be lured and bred using carrots. Rabbits can be lured and bred with carrots, golden carrots or dandelions.

Once two animals breed, a baby version will spawn and the two parent animals will be unable to enter love mode again for approximately five minutes. It takes around 20 minutes for the baby to become full grown, at which point it will become available for breeding.

In order to lure or breed chickens, it's exactly the same

process, but instead you must use seeds. They can be wheat seeds, which are the easiest to find and are the only seeds you can use to lure a chicken, but you may also use pumpkin seeds, melon seeds or Nether wart to breed them. Pumpkin and melon seeds can be crafted from the fruits they produce. To find out how this is done, turn to the Crafting Glossary, or to learn where to find Nether wart check out The Nether.

Two sheep and a lamb

ENCLOSURES

One of the most important things to note about enclosures is that they aren't always as effective as you may hope. For example, when keeping animals enclosed, your animal mustn't be able to move more than 20 blocks in any given direction, as this will allow it to despawn at random. For this reason, it is wise to make your animal enclosure no more than 20x20.

Some animals will wait by gates and try to escape when you enter. This can be avoided by fencing around gates and entry points. For example, if you have an enclosure with a gate, add an extra area of fencing around each gate and install another gate. This gives you the opportunity to close the first gate behind you and contain any escapees.

You can enclose animals in other ways, such as building walls and installing doors. However, if your enclosure should become over-populated, animals can be pushed through solid blocks, causing them to suffocate and die. If this happens with fencing, the animal is simply pushed through the fence and remains unharmed. For this reason, it's important not to over-populate your enclosures.

If you decide to use fencing, it's important to note that creatures can jump from adjacent blocks onto and across your fence. This is usually only done when there is a block next to or one block away from your fence. If you're unsure of your fence's security, try jumping across yourself. If you can't cross, it's likely that nothing else will be able to either. If you're building fences up- or downhill, build it higher wherever there's a block higher around it and do so for at least two blocks along your fence, as this can sometimes allow things to jump across. And, as has already been mentioned, aggressive mobs don't like light and, as long as the area in and around your fence is well lit, these mobs won't spawn within your fence's perimeter.

Always remember that sheep specifically require grass, but other animals can be kept on whichever material you wish to build on, and they usually do quite well regardless of the ground beneath them. Try not to keep baby animals around water as they can't swim and may drown. If you wish to keep water in your enclosures, it's good to breed animals in separate enclosures until they're fully grown.

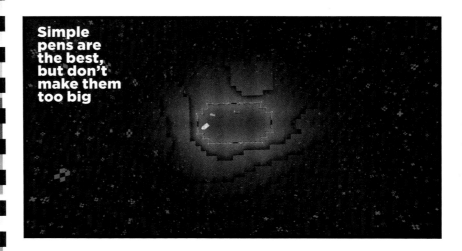
Simple pens are the best, but don't make them too big

ANIMAL TAMING

Most mobs in Minecraft want to eat or kill you, but some can be friendly, if you know how to befriend them

Minecraft's mobs are a rather angry bunch and, if you see something moving, you can bet it usually wants to do you harm. However, you can not only get some mobs to like you, but they'll also carry you around and even fight for you.

There are four different tameable mobs currently in the game (not including utility mobs like the snow and iron golem). These mobs begin as friendly, but they still behave differently, and taming them isn't easy.

WOLVES

Wolves are the most common tameable mobs in the game, and can be found in forest and taiga (snow forest) biomes. Unlike the other tameable mods, wolves can become enraged and attack if provoked, along with any pack members nearby, so be careful.

To tame a wolf, all you need to do is approach one and feed it a bone. A bone has a one in three chance of taming a wolf. Once

tamed, wolves become dogs and have a red (dyeable) collar. Dogs have over twice the health of a wolf, and hit twice as hard.

Dogs can follow the player and will attack anything that attacks their master. They can be told to sit and won't move until told to do so, making them excellent guard dogs. If a dog is left behind and isn't sitting (such as getting stuck on a fence or underground), they can automatically teleport to their owner's position, so you don't need to worry about losing them.

They can, like most mobs in the game, drown in water, suffer damage (or death) from falling, and can be killed by fire and lava. Of course, they also take damage in combat, and their current health level is denoted by the angle of their tail.

PIGS

Although not tameable in the same way as other mobs, with a saddle and some carrots you can use them as transport.

To ride a pig, you'll first need a saddle. These can't be crafted, but can be found in abandoned mineshaft, dungeons, Nether fortresses and temples. You can also trade saddles with villagers, and they can sometimes be found in blacksmith's chests.

You'll then need to craft a carrot on a

Just give a wolf a bone (or a few) to tame it

OCELOTS

Ocelots are cats found only in jungle biomes, and are the most difficult mob to tame due to their timid, wary nature. However, it's worth the hassle, as tamed ocelots become cats and are the only thing that can actually scare away creepers, making them perfect home defenders. Ocelots are one of the fastest mobs in the game, and can sprint very quickly, which can make taming them difficult if not done correctly.

To tame an ocelot, you'll need some raw

Ocelots are timid, but once tamed and turned into cats they're perfect creeper defence

fish (possibly as many as 20) and the right tactics. Holding the raw fish, you'll need to locate an ocelot (keep the fish in your hand at all times and walk slowly, don't run). When you find one, it has to approach you of its own accord; you can't chase it. You'll need to do this in an open area too. Ocelots feel threatened in confined spaces, so taming won't work.

HORSES

The most recent tameable mob is the horse, a ridable beast that can be essential for long journeys. Horses, and their donkey variations, spawn only in the plains biome and need to be tamed before you can ride them.

Horses are a versatile ally, and easy enough to tame

Horses are one of the fastest means of travel in the game, have a very high jump ability (they can even jump fences), and can be equipped with horse armour. Donkeys and mules can be equipped with chests, making them useful for transporting items.

To tame a horse, you'll need a saddle and some patience. Unlike the other mobs, you don't feed a horse to tame it, but attempt to ride it. To do so, approach a horse with an empty hand and use it. You then need to saddle it.

stick, to control the pig. To do so, use a fishing rod and a carrot. This can be done without a crafting table. Now, saddle and jump on.

The pig will head in the direction you point the carrot. As you ride, the pig will eat the carrot, the status of which is shown by the durability bar. If you use the carrot on a stick, the pig will run faster for a short time, but this uses a quarter of the carrot. Once a carrot is fully eaten, you'll be left with a fishing rod, and you'll need to make another carrot.

Saddle a pig and you've got a speedy, pink ride

COOKBOOK

Your hunger bar isn't something to ignore. You very quickly realise that all that block-breaking and potion-making works up a hefty appetite. This becomes very apparent when you're in the middle of an epic siege and your stomach begins to groan louder than the zombies at your door. Whether you're a food critic or not, that hunger bar simply must be replenished in order for you to survive. Below is a list of the culinary cuisine the Minecraft world has to offer. Gordon Ramsay, eat your heart out!

THE HUNGER GAME

The first thing to note is that without food you can't fill your hunger bar, which appears alongside your health bar as 10 drumsticks. These drumsticks will deplete with everything you do. Some actions will drain your hunger bar quicker than others. For example, sprinting causes your hunger bar to deplete quicker over a shorter amount of time than walking does and, in fact, you can't sprint if your hunger bar is below three drumsticks.

The most important purpose of food and the hunger bar is heartily illustrated when you can no longer regenerate health. If your hunger bar shows less than nine full drumsticks, your health bar can't refill. This makes food an inescapable part of surviving, no matter what your eventual goal may be. If your food bar reaches zero, it will begin to shiver and your health bar will deplete either until you eat something or it reaches zero and you die.

It's wise to carry food with you on long journeys, if you're mining, or if there's a chance you'll get injured or stuck in one place for some time. Alternatively, you can look for food while you're out and about; however, food can be scarce, especially underground, so plan ahead.

FRUIT AND VEG

Apple

An apple will replenish up to two drumsticks of your bar. They're dropped from the leaves of oak trees either as you cut them or as they die. Apples can also be found in stronghold chests, bonus chests, and blacksmiths chests found in NPC villages.

Golden apple

Golden apples are rare but very valuable. They restore up to two drumsticks of your health and also have added benefits. They possess the power of regeneration. A golden apple will initially regenerate your health for five seconds. They also cause absorption for two minutes. Absorption is a status effect that provides another two hearts on top of any existing health you have (including the hearts you regained in the first five seconds); however, the extra two hearts will only last as long as the absorption effect is active.

Enchanted golden apple

The enchanted golden apple also has the ability to restore your health as well as your hunger bar. They are, however, much more powerful. They restore the initial two drumsticks of hunger like red and golden apples, but they also regenerate your health for up to 30 seconds (as opposed to five seconds for a normal golden apple), although this is a slower form of regeneration. The enchanted golden apple provides absorption for two minutes, but also grants you resistance and fire resistance. Resistance reduces all damage you take by 20%, and fire resistance provides immunity to fire and lava. Both last for five minutes and can prove useful when coming in contact with creatures like the blaze.

Melon

Melon slices restore one drumstick of your hunger bar each and can be combined with eight golden nuggets (in the same way that you make a golden apple) to make glistering melon, which is a key ingredient in potion making. Melon seeds are initially found in abandoned mine shafts. From those first seeds you can grow melon blocks. Melon or melon slices (the edible form of the fruit) are dropped by destroying the melon blocks. Usually you can get up to seven slices per block. If you don't wish to eat your slices, you can craft them back into blocks, which requires nine slices, or craft more seeds out of them.

Carrot

Carrots restore two drumsticks of hunger, can be farmed and pigs love them! Carrots can be dropped by zombies, found in village crops, or they can be grown. You don't need to harvest seeds from a carrot, but use the carrot itself to plant more. You can plant them by selecting a carrot, aiming at a farmed block and using it. PC users can use carrots to lure and breed pigs, and with the aid of a carrot and a fishing rod, can ride a pig.

Golden carrot

A golden carrot restores three drumsticks of hunger and prevents you from getting hungry again for longer than other foods. They have to be crafted and can't be found. Unlike the golden apple, it doesn't provide restoration, absorption, or resistance of any kind. However, the golden carrot shows its full potential both in potion brewing and its use in the breeding of horses, mules and donkeys.

Potato

A single potato restores one drumstick of your hunger bar and can be baked to create a baked potato. Potatoes are difficult to find. They can be dropped by zombies and grow in NPC villages just as carrots do. Once you have your potato, you can farm it. Like carrots, potatoes are planted directly into a farmed block. You don't need to harvest seeds from a potato in order to farm it. As well as dropping normal potatoes, a matured potato crop will very rarely drop an extra poisonous potato.

Baked potato

A baked potato is simply a normal potato cooked in a furnace. A baked potato will restore up to three drumsticks of your hunger bar. You can use any kind of fuel in your furnace as long as it burns and it will still produce a baked potato. Baked potatoes can't be found or traded.

Mushroom stew

Mushroom stew (also known as mushroom soup) fills three drumsticks of your hunger bar and is currently the only way to eat mushrooms. Mushrooms can be found under trees, close to swamps and in mushroom biomes. Mushrooms also grow in the Nether. If you use bone meal on a planted mushroom, it will turn into a huge mushroom. When each block of a huge mushroom is destroyed, it may then drop many normal-sized mushrooms as a result.

Mushroom stew is only available by crafting or by milking a mooshroom (for an infinite supply), and in order to do either of these things you must first craft yourself a bowl.

Once you have a bowl, you can craft mushroom stew by placing a bowl in your crafting screen along with both types of mushroom. The placement doesn't matter; as long as you have both red and brown mushrooms and a bowl, this will craft one bowl of stew.

MEAT

Raw beef

You get raw beef by killing cows (including mooshrooms) and it fills just less than two drumsticks of your hunger bar. It's one of the easiest foods to get hold of, especially if you farm animals. Steak is raw beef's cooked form, and is more beneficial as it fills more of your hunger bar.

Raw pork chops

Raw pork is obtained by killing pigs and restores just less than two drumsticks of hunger. It can also be cooked in a furnace to make cooked pork chops.

Raw chicken

Raw chicken is dropped by chickens when killed and restores one drumstick on the hunger bar. It also has a 30% chance of causing food poisoning, which is why it's best to cook chicken in a furnace before eating.

Raw fish

Raw fish are caught using a fishing rod and restore one drumstick on your hunger bar. They can be used to tame ocelots but don't have any effect on tamed wolves. You can find different breeds of fish, including normal fish, salmon, clownfish and pufferfish. All raw fish refills one drumstick of hunger. Pufferfish also causes Nausea II, Poison IV, and Hunger III, so it's best avoided.

Raw rabbit

Raw rabbit is dropped by rabbits and restores two drumsticks of hunger when consumed.

Raw mutton

Raw mutton is dropped by sheep when killed. If consumed, it refills one drumstick of the hunger bar. Raw beef, pork chops, rabbit, mutton, and chicken can all be used to lure, breed and heal tamed wolves.

Steak

Also known as cooked beef, steak is simply raw beef cooked in a furnace and is the more nourishing form of beef, restoring up to four drumsticks of your hunger bar.

Another way to obtain steak is to set a living cow (or mooshroom) on fire. You can do this by using flint and steel to set fire to the blocks surrounding the animal, or by making one walk into fire or lava. Any beef that is dropped as it dies will be ready cooked.

Cooked pork chops

This is just a raw pork chop that has been cooked in a furnace and restores four drumsticks of hunger, much like steak. You can set pigs on fire too, as with cows.

Cooked chicken

Cooked chicken is raw chicken that has been cooked in a furnace, much like steak and pork chops. It restores three drumsticks of hunger and won't poison you. Chickens can also be killed using fire to produce ready cooked chicken.

Cooked mutton

Cooked mutton can be created in a furnace, and when eaten it will refill three drumsticks of your hunger bar.

Cooked rabbit

Cooked rabbit is made in a furnace, and when eaten it will restore three drumsticks of your hunger bar.

Like their raw counterparts, steak, cooked pork chops, cooked rabbit, cooked mutton, and cooked chicken can also be used to lure, breed and heal tamed wolves.

Cooked fish

Cooked normal fish is raw fish that has been cooked in a furnace and restores just less than three drumsticks of your hunger bar. Cooked salmon restore a full three drumsticks. You can't cook clownfish or pufferfish.

Unlike raw fish, cooked fish can't be used to tame ocelots.

Rabbit stew

One of the best healing items you can cook, rabbit stew is created using cooked rabbit, a mushroom, a potato, a carrot, and a wooden bowl. When eaten, it will refill ten drumsticks of your hunger bar, with very high (12) staturation. After eating, you'll get an empty bowl.

BAKERY

Bread

Bread is straightforward. It's a great way to utilise wheat when you're not using it to lure and breed your livestock. Three bales of wheat in your crafting screen make one loaf of bread, which restores just less than three drumsticks of your hunger bar.

Cookies

Cookies are crafted in batches of eight, and each cookie restores one drumstick of hunger.

Cookies are comprised of two bales of wheat and one lot of cocoa beans. Cocoa beans can be found in cocoa pods, which grow in the jungle biomes on the sides of trees. When a cocoa pod is broken at full maturity, it will drop up to three lots of cocoa beans. Cocoa beans can also be found in dungeon chests.

Pumpkin pie

Pumpkin pie is made using a pumpkin, sugar and an egg, and restores up to four drumsticks of your hunger bar.

Sugar can be crafted from sugar cane by simply placing harvested sugar cane in one slot of your crafting screen. A pumpkin can be grown or found in the plains and mountain biomes, and eggs are laid by chickens. Pumpkin pie can be crafted by placing sugar, an egg and a pumpkin in your crafting screen in no particular slots or order.

Cake

A whole cake is the only block that's edible and can't be eaten whilst held. It must first be placed, and once placed can't be moved. You can then eat it by aiming at it and selecting use. There'll be no eating animation; a slice of cake simply disappears and your hunger bar will be replenished automatically. A whole cake consists of a total of seven slices and can be shared among players. Each slice replenishes one drumstick of hunger, so eating a whole cake restores up to six drumsticks.

POISONS

Poisonous potato

Poisonous potatoes are sometimes dropped when harvesting a potato crop. Poisonous potatoes can't be planted or baked and inflict poison if eaten. Poison turns your health bar to a yellow colour and continually damages you until the poison wears off. The poisonous potato restores two drumsticks of your hunger bar, but at your own risk. You have a 60% chance of losing a heart of your health bar when you eat a poisonous potato. Beware when harvesting potato crops, as a poisonous potato doesn't differ very much in appearance to a normal one.

Spider eye

A spider eye restores one drumstick of hunger, but will always poison you for four seconds at a time, costing you two hearts of health. Spider eyes are dropped when you kill spiders and cave spiders. They aren't dropped when spiders die naturally. Spider eyes can also be dropped by witches. A spider eye is key when making fermented spider eyes and can be used in potion brewing.

Rotten flesh

Rotten flesh is dropped by zombies and zombie pigmen, and can restore up to two drumsticks of your hunger bar. However, rotten flesh has an 80% chance of inflicting food poisoning. Food poisoning turns your hunger bar a green-yellow colour and drains your hunger much quicker than usual, making everyday things like walking more exhausting. It lasts up to 30 seconds and can be eased by drinking milk. Rotten flesh can be fed to tamed wolves and won't cause any poisoning or damage to them. This makes healing wolves less wasteful.

THE LAY OF THE LAND: A GUIDE TO MINECRAFT'S BIOMES

When playing Minecraft, you'll notice that the land is divided up into distinct sections: deserts, swampland, forests and more. Alone, these sections are referred to as a separate 'biome'. There are 61 unique biomes, split into five main categories, and each one has its own characteristics, which are worth learning so you know where to go for the resource you're after. Here are some of the main biome types.

FOREST

Forest biomes are composed of small clumps of deciduous trees – oak and birch – as well as flowers and mushrooms. Many animals roam here, but you're likely to find wolves. They make a good starting point due to the amount of wood and simple terrain. The forest biome is among the smallest – you're unlikely to see anything the size of a desert.

DESERT

Deserts are vast biomes carpeted in sand and free from most animals and plant life. Sugar cane will grow here if there's water nearby, and it's the only biome where cacti and dead bushes appear. Deserts are huge and often home to villages. It won't rain here, but there can be naturally occurring water. Unsurprisingly, this is where you'll find desert temples.

PLAINS

Plains are large, mostly flat areas with long grass, which often obscures lakes and ravines. Villages are commonly found here and they're the only area in which horses spawn. The abundance of grass makes them ideal for collecting seeds.

SWAMPLAND

Swamps are recognisable by their mix of dark-green islands and shallow, greenish water filled with lily pads. Vines hang off any trees, and mushrooms are abundant. Swamps are a good place to find clay, and the only place where witch huts are generated.

JUNGLE / RAINFOREST

The jungle biome consists of tall, thick trees with dense leaf cover. There are several unique features – cocoa pods can be found hanging off trees, ocelots naturally spawn here, and they're the only biome that generates ferns. Trees are normally covered in vines, which can be scaled. You'll also find jungle temples in this biome.

EXTREME HILLS

Extreme hills are very steep. Expect cliffs, valleys, outcrops and mad scenery. This is the only biome where you can find emerald ore and silverfish are naturally generated.

TAIGA

Mountainous with snow and ice, and a large number of tall, conical evergreens called spruce trees. Wolves are common.

OCEAN

Oceans are huge bodies of water that are difficult to traverse without a boat. The sea floor tends to be composed of dirt and sand, and resembles a collection of mountains and plains formed below sea level. Squid are common and you can find ocean monuments.

MUSHROOM ISLAND

The rarest biome of all, mushroom islands are only found adjacent to ocean biomes and are topped with mycelium rather than dirt. Mushrooms are abundant, and they're the only area to generate huge mushrooms and mooshrooms, the fungus-infected cow mob. No other mobs will spawn here, making underground exploration especially safe.

OTHER ENVIRONMENTS

As well as the ten biomes listed here, there are other variants (beaches, flower forests, roofed forest, and so on) and two other main ones, which aren't part of the Overworld: the Nether and the End. These are only reachable under certain conditions and are covered elsewhere in this guide. Although this guide might help you learn the more useful qualities, it can't convey the fun of exploring each biome and learning its features.

ICE PLAINS / TUNDRA

Ice plains are large, flat biomes covered in snow. All surface water is frozen into ice, and instead of rain, it snows. Oak trees are sparsely dotted around, but wood is scarce. There are no unique animals or structures to be found, because, let's face it, who would want to live here?

MINECARTS

For a game that's allegedly about mining, Minecraft makes few allowances to the practical realities of the activity. You don't need to prop up shafts, worry about gas pockets, or protest against government cuts to your industry. But one thing you can do is create systems of minecarts to transfer both you and your spoils across great distances.

We'll give you all the information you need to create your own minecart railway, and explain how best to use it. Whether you just want to get your hard-won treasures back to base without a long trek, or plan to build a scenic cliff-side roller-coaster journey for your friends, you can learn everything right here.

A powered train with different types of cart

TYPES OF MINECART

As well as the basic empty minecart, which players can ride in, there are four item combinations that create minecarts with unique properties:

The **storage minecart** is a combination of chest and minecart, and is used to transfer and store goods. Destroying a storage minecart will spill its contents in the same way destroying a chest would. The game's physics treats storage minecarts identically to empty ones, regardless of what's contained within them.

The **powered minecart** is made by placing a stone furnace inside a minecart. When loaded with fuel (charcoal or coal), they can be used to push other minecarts as an alternative to redstone-powered rails. A single unit of fuel will power the minecart for three minutes, covering a maximum of 612 blocks. They're relatively weak, however, and are unable to push player-occupied minecarts up 1/1 inclines unless there are at least two available (you can chain a maximum of three to provide a more powerful engine).

The **hopper minecart** is a minecart containing an item hopper, which can collect items it comes in contact with, or from containers directly above it. The hopper can be switched on and off using redstone-powered activator rails. They're useful for clearing passages of collected material or setting up systems of automated transfer.

Finally, the **TNT minecart** is an explosive cart made by crafting an empty minecart with TNT. Although it can be moved manually without danger, a TNT-filled cart will explode if it hits an activator rail, derails and moves more than three blocks, is destroyed while in motion, or ignited by fire damage.

TIPS & TRICKS

Due to the way distance in the Nether corresponds to distance in the Overworld, you can save resources by combining rail systems with portals. Where rails cross, minecart behaviour is hard-wired to force them to travel either south or east, whichever is perpendicular to their current direction.

The exception is if any rails lead downhill.

Mobs won't cross rails unless they're chasing the player (or food), so rails can be used to 'fence off' areas from non-aggressive entities without obstructing the movement of players.

Due to the way minecart speeds are calculated, they travel fastest when moving diagonally. Minecarts moving diagonally can travel eight blocks a second on both the X and Z axis, creating an effective speed of 11.3 blocks a second. Mobs that are pushed into rideable minecarts will automatically enter and remain until displaced by the player or until the game is quit, at which point they exit the cart.

Storage minecart

Powered minecart

Hopper minecart

TNT minecart

TYPES OF RAIL

Minecarts travel along rails, which can be found underground in abandoned mines, or crafted by players using iron and a stick. If a minecart runs out of track, it can roll along flat ground, but will become fragile and snap to any rails it encounters. There are several types of rail that are useful in creating complex and automated minecart systems:

Powered rail

Detector rail

The **powered rail** is made using gold, a stick and redstone, and can stop or boost minecarts, depending on the status of its redstone power (off = stop, on = boost). Sufficiently fast minecarts can pass through off-state powered rails, but will be badly slowed. The **detector rail** is crafted using iron, redstone and a pressure plate not a stick. They'll behave the same way as a pressure plate, generating a redstone signal when a minecart passes over them. Finally, an **activator rail** is made by crafting iron, two sticks and a redstone torch. These rails are purely used for activating carts that pass over them, which in practice means switching a hopper minecart on or off, and igniting the fuse on TNT minecarts. When in their off state, they act as a normal piece of track and have no other effects.

NPC VILLAGES

Although Minecraft's worlds are largely uninhabited, there are signs of civilization, and villages, complete with inhabitants, can be found

Minecraft started out life as a fairly lonely place; that's if you don't count the army of nasties out for your blood. However, eventually the game introduced NPC villages. These ready-made towns contain various buildings, roads and villagers to trade with.

NPC villages can be hard to find and don't always occur in a console world, so, if playing on console, there's no guarantee that your newly generated terrain will house an NPC village. You can go on an epic quest on PC to find NPC villages, and it can take some time in the almost endless world. There are tricks to finding them, though.

WHERE'S THAT TOWN?

If you're having trouble even finding an NPC village, there are a few things to note that may be of help. First and foremost, NPC villages only occur in plains or desert biomes. They can't be found in any other biome.

Villages can spawn in strange places, even on top of huge chasms

Villages in the desert feature sandstone buildings, whilst wood and stone are the materials of choice for grassland dwellers.

On the PC, NPC villages will spawn more often in worlds that feature large biomes, so be sure to select this world option. If you simply can't find a village in a normal or large biome world, you can utilise a small trick. Please note, however, this won't always work.

First, in your current world, find your seed code. You can do this by going to the chat window and typing '/seed'. Note this code down, then create a brand new superflat world using the same seed.

Villages offer shelter and trade, but are far from safe

Once in the world, fly around it to find a village. If and when you do, on the PC press F3 to get the coordinates. Now, load up your original world and go to those same coordinates. Occasionally, this will reveal a village at the same location. Different biome types can prevent this, though. You can try the same trick again, but instead of selecting a superflat world use a default world.

Of course, you can also simply go into Creative mode, select large biomes (on PC) and fly around to easily find a village. You can then change the game mode to the one you like and carry on (with cheats active, go into chat and type '/gamemode X', where X is the game mode you want).

THIS OL' TOWN

Villages aren't all created equal, and they'll often have different configurations of buildings. Some will have more types of building than others. These buildings come from a selection of possibles, which you'll find listed here...

Blacksmith
Contains a chest with random goodies, furnaces and a lava pool. The blacksmith spawns here.

Butcher
Spawns a butcher.

Church
Spawns a priest and sometimes a farmer.

Farm
Spawns in small or large, and contains plots of crops, including carrots, potatoes and wheat.

Hut
Spawns a villager.

Large house
Spawns two farmers.

Library
Holds bookcases and a crafting table. Also spawns a librarian and a farmer.

Small house
Spawns a villager but has no door, so is not considered an actual house by villagers.

Guardtower
Spawns a farmer, but with no door isn't an actual house.

Well
Not an actual building, but a source of water.

SIEGE MENTALITY

Players stumbling into villages may thank their lucky stars, as finding a host of pre-made buildings and people living in them may present a feeling of safety and hope. Sadly, in Minecraft this isn't entirely true.

Whilst finding a village is a definite plus, as it opens up trading and decent buildings to seek refuge in, villagers, although friendly, are about as useful in a fight as a paper sword in the rain. They have no combat ability, and won't help you out if you're under attack.

This is because most mobs don't notice villagers, and the one that does only sends them fleeing into their houses. This mob is the zombie.

An important part of any Minecraft game that involves villagers and trading is defence against zombie sieges. At night, villages can often come under attack from zombie hordes, and the denizens' only defence against them is to run away and hide, and often their relative lack of intelligence doesn't even let them do this. Villagers can be easily caught by zombies and killed, turning then into zombified villagers. This not only creates more enemies for you to fight, but reduces your trading options at the same time.

Larger villages will often have iron golems guarding them, which can help greatly, but not all do. And, even with a golem on the prowl, the sheer number of attacking zombies can quickly overwhelm a village, rendering it a ghost town after a while.

Remember: on harder modes, zombies can break down wooden doors, so even in their homes villagers aren't always safe. Therefore, it's a good idea to help out these unfortunate souls.

MAKIN' THE STREETS SAFE

If you find a village and value your relations with it, you may want to consider giving it your help. This means outfitting the village with defences to prevent as much damage as possible from attack.

There are all manner of tactics you can use, many of which you'll probably already use for your own home base. Building a wall around the town can stop other mobs from joining in, as they'll spawn if you're around.

They may not attack the villagers, but a creeper explosion will cause all sorts of havoc. Keep them out to protect against this.

Bathe the entire village and the surrounding area in light, including the rooftops. This stops spawning and can greatly help to thin out your woes.

If you've got some wolves to spare (and ocelots if you have them for creeper repulsion), place them around the village at key points. They can help defend the village. If you have the materials to build an iron golem for the village, do so. If they already have one, build more. Numbers always help.

Sadly, zombie sieges often spawn zombies in the village itself, so walls and other traditional defences don't always work. So, turn your attention to blocking in individual houses, making sure the inhabitants are inside beforehand, of course.

Zombies can't jump to hit a door, and if they can't reach the whole door they can't break it down, so ensure the doors open outwards and remove any stairs from the front of houses. This will prevent zombies getting in as they'll only break down half the door. Sadly, villagers can't use or even recognise iron doors, so they're not an option. They're also ignored when it comes to spawning/breeding rules (more on this later).

If you repel an attack, ensure you check all defences are still okay, including doors and the health of any wolves and golems in order to keep the village safe for the next assault.

Zombie villagers can be cured, so put away that sword and help

MEDIC!

If any villagers have been converted into zombies during a siege, all hope isn't lost, and they can be restored. There are two methods of curing zombification in villagers. The first is to use a potion of weakness, and the second is to feed them a golden apple (made with gold ingots). Once done, you'll hear a loud noise, the villager will vibrate and emit red swirls, signifying success. You then have to wait several minutes for the cure to take effect. The problem with this is the flammable nature of zombies in sunlight. This also afflicts zombie villagers, and if you don't take precautions they'll be extra crispy before they're cured. They're also stronger in this state, so extra care needs to be taken.

For this reason, you should lure the infected villager into a house, then seal it up. This stops them getting out, and other villagers from getting in and being attacked. Ensure no daylight can get in, and also barricade doors to stop zombies getting in and your patient from getting out.

Alternatively, simply build an impromptu structure, lead the zombified villager in, and block them up until the cure works (you'll hear the familiar villager muttering). When cured, villagers can go about their business and can once again breed, repopulating the village.

MR POPULAR

Although this isn't Fable, villagers do have a popularity rating of you, and this can increase or decrease depending on your actions. To increase your popularity, trade with villagers. Attacking and killing villagers, especially children (you monster!) will decrease your rating. Killing the village's iron golem, if it has one, will decrease your rating even more.

As of version 1.8.6, popularity serves no purpose other than causing a village's iron golem(s) to attack you if your rating drops to -15 or below. Popularity is measured by each village, so you can be one village's best friend and another's worst enemy. Below are the actions that can affect your popularity rating.

Player action	Popularity rating change
Trading last offer slot item	+1
Attacking a villager	-1
Killing a villager	-2
Attacking a child	-3
Destroying an iron golem	-5

VILLAGER TRADING

Presuming you've gone through all the hassles of protecting a village from zombie sieges and keeping its inhabitants alive, you'll probably want something back for your efforts. Let's face it, you're certainly not going to get repaid in stimulating conversation.

Luckily, villagers, although not exactly blessed with charming personalities, are good sources of items. You can trade with them to make it easier to get some of the game's more difficult-to-find resources, and to acquire enchanted items without having to go through the hassle of creating your own enchanting table.

Trading requires plenty of emeralds, as well as items that each villager profession can use (which they'll buy in return for emeralds). Through this system, you can acquire some items that can be very hard to get your hands on otherwise, such as chainmail, and you can also grab the elusive bottle 'o' enchanting in Survival mode using this method.

Those big noses can smell a bargain, and villagers love to trade

TRADING BEHAVIOUR

Trading with a village can take some time to fully evolve into a useful marketplace, and only by performing numerous trades with all of the various inhabitants will you garner the most out of the trading system.

Each villager will initially have only one offer for you, but as you trade with them they'll generate different offers. This is achieved by trading their last (or right-most) offer. Villagers will only offer items at a set price and quantity, and only one offer for an item will be available at any one time. So if a farmer is selling eight apples, he'll only sell eight for the requested price and not seven, unless a new offer is generated that replaces the previous one. When a villager creates a new offer, they'll emit a brief aura, similar to the visual indicator generated when you cure one of zombification.

Villagers can have many offers at any one time, but you can't simply keep using the same offer to stock up. Once a trade has been used more than three times, it's eligible for deactivation (unless it's the only offer available that's still active). The number of trades it takes to deactivate an offer is random, but if it reaches 13 it will always be stopped (again, unless it's the last possible offer).

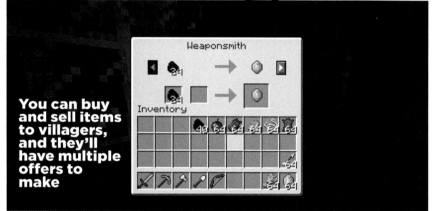

You can buy and sell items to villagers, and they'll have multiple offers to make

GETTING THE GREEN

Trading depends almost exclusively on emeralds, so if you're going to set up negotiation with the local settlement, you'll need to find and bring plenty of them. The problem is, as all valuable things usually are, they're quite hard to find.

Emeralds can be mined just like other ores, but you're less likely to find them. They can usually be found in extreme hills biomes in singular

numbers, and also crop up in desert and jungle biomes inside temples. Emeralds are used almost exclusively for trading, with their only other uses being in beacons and for decoration. Once mined, emerald ore is smelted in the usual way to create emerald gems.

VILLAGERS AND THEIR WARES

Villagers come in five different colours (with the sixth, basic villager not usually generated), and each colour has different professions, each of which makes different offers when trading and accepts different item for emeralds. For example, the farmer will sell you various foodstuffs and will gladly pay you emeralds for pumpkins, melons and wheat. The cleric, on the other hand, sells eyes of ender and will buy gold ingots.

To trade with a villager, simply approach them and use them to open the trading interface. Then, place your items, either goods to trade or emeralds to pay with, into the left-hand box. When you place the required number of items in the boxes, the item to buy or emeralds will appear in the right-hand box and can be placed into your inventory.

Below you'll find details of each villager's trades and their prices. These are all in emeralds unless specified, as some items also require additional items alongside emeralds. The quantities needed for each sale or the amount you get in a purchase are also listed.

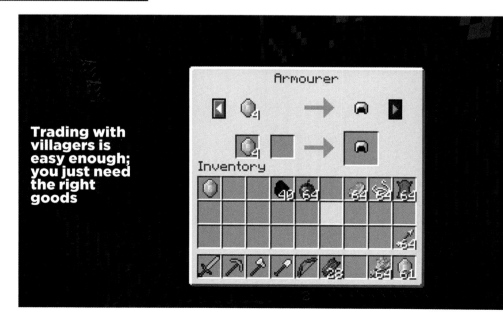

Trading with villagers is easy enough; you just need the right goods

BROWN ROBES

Farmers sell cooked and prepared food; buy wheat and veg. Fishermen sell cooked fish, rods; buy string, coal. Shepherds sell shears, dyed wool; buy white wool. Fletchers sell bows, arrows, flint; buy string.

Buys	
Item	Price
Farmer	
Wheat	1 (for 18-22 units)
Potato	1 (for 15-19 potatoes)
Carrot	1 (for 15-19 carrots)
Pumpkin	1 (for 8-13 pumpkins)
Melon	1 (for 7-12 melons)
Fisherman	
String	1 (for 15-20 units)
Coal	1 (for 16-24 lumps)
Shepherd	
White wool	1 (for 16-22 blocks)
Fletcher	
String	1 (for 15-20 units)

Sells	
Item	Price
Farmer	
Bread	1 (for 2-4 loaves)
Pumpkin pie	1 (for 2-3 pies)
Apple	1 (for 5 apples)
Cookie	1 (for 6 cookies)
Cake	1
Fisherman	
Cooked Fish	6 fish and 1 emerald (for 6 cooked fish)
Enchanted rod	7-8
Shepherd	
Shears	3-4
Coloured wool	1-2 (per block)
Fletcher	
Arrow	1 (for 8-12 arrows)
Bow	2-3
Flint	10 gravel and 1 emerald (for 6-10 pieces)

CLERIC (PURPLE ROBE)

One of the more useful villagers, the cleric sells eyes of ender and other rare items, including the bottle 'o' enchanting.

Buys	
Item	Price
Rotten flesh	1 (for 36-40)
Gold ingot	1 (for 8-10 ingots)

Sells	
Bottle 'o' enchanting	3-11
Eye of ender	7-11
Glowstone	1 (for 1-3 units)
Redstone	1 (for 1-4 units)
Lapis lazuli	1 (for 1-2 units)

LIBRARIAN (WHITE ROBE)

These bookworm villagers specialise in, what else? Books. They also sell enchanted books and other tools.

Sells	
Item	Price
Bookshelf	3
Clock	10-11
Compass	10-11
Enchanted book	5-64 and 1 book
Glass	1 (for 3-5 panes)
Name tag	20-22

WHITE APRON

Butchers buy and sell meat. Leatherworkers sell leather armour and saddles. If you have a big enough farm for meat and leather, they're a good

Buys	
Item	Price
Butcher	
Raw porkchop	1 (for 14-18 chops)
Raw chicken	1 (for 14-18 chickens)
Coal	1 (for 16-24 lumps)
Leatherworker	
Leather	1 (for 9-12 hides)

Sells	
Item	Price (per item)
Butcher	
Cooked porkchop	1 (for 5-7 chops)
Cooked chicken	1 (for 6-8 chickens)
Leatherworker	
Enchanted leather tunic	7-12
Leather pants	2-4
Saddle	8-10

Buys	
Item	Price
Book	1 (for 8-10 books)
Paper	1 (for 24-36 sheets)
Written book	1 (for 2 books)

BLACK APRON

These are armourers, weaponsmiths, and toolsmiths. They sell tools, armour and weapons making them an easy source of replacements.

Buys	
All variants buy the same items at the same prices	
Coal	1
Diamond	1
Gold Ingot	1

Sells	
Item	Price (per item)
Armourer	
Iron helmet	4-6
Iron chestplate	10-14
Chainmail chestplate	11-15
Chainmail leggings	9-11
Chainmail boots	5-7
Chainmail helmet	5-7
Enchanted diamond chestplate	16-19
Weaponsmith	
Iron axe	6-8
Enchanted iron sword	9-10
Ench. diamond axe	9-12
Enchanted diamond sword	12-15
Toolsmith	
Enchanted iron shovel	5-7
Enchanted iron pickaxe	9-11
Enchanted diamond pickaxe	12-15

VILLAGER

Only spawnable using console commands or mods, and not naturally, the rank-and-file villager (who wears green clothes) doesn't really trade as such, but they'll buy gold ingots off you for one emerald apiece.

Minecraft might be filled with hostile forces, but that doesn't mean you're left unprotected. There are many ways you can defend yourself, but the best way to progress is to go on the offensive. Learning how to handle yourself in a fight will dramatically extend your life and give you the chance to collect all sorts of rare items – some rewards are only available for successfully defeating a mob, while others are much easier to steal from a felled enemy than make yourself!

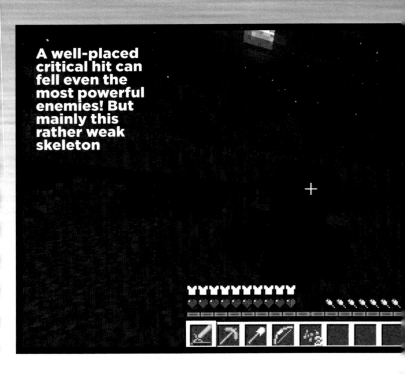

A well-placed critical hit can fell even the most powerful enemies! But mainly this rather weak skeleton

SWORDPLAY: FIGHTING TECHNIQUES

WEAPONS

The selection of weapons in Minecraft is actually quite small, with only two dedicated weapons in the entire game: a sword and a bow and arrow. You can use other items to deal damage (axes are reasonably good at this) and you can brew damage-dealing potions, or even use a flint and steel to cause fire damage, but only the sword allows you to block, and only the bow and arrow allows you to deal significant ranged damage.

The most powerful and durable sword in the game is, by a huge margin, the diamond sword, which deals 8 damage and can make over 1,000 kills before it wears out. The more common iron sword is the second best, dealing 7 damage and making only 100 or so kills before breaking. Bows require ammunition in the form of arrows, but a direct hit from a fully drawn bow does the most damage – 9, or sometimes even 10 points. Arrows can be retrieved after being fired and used repeatedly, but bows will break after firing 385 times, assuming durability is lost no other way.

BLOCKING & BLOCK-HITTING

Blocking is an important skill to learn. Using a sword to block (no other object in the game allows blocking) will prevent the player receiving 50% of the damage caused by many types of attack, including arrows and explosions. Although blocking doesn't decrease a sword's durability, it does cause the player to move much slower to prevent over-use. Learning to block attacks is a useful skill.

Rapidly blocking and attacking (called block-hitting) will 'short-cut' the animation, allowing attacks to be dealt much faster than simply attacking in quick succession.

Blocking protects against damage from arrows and explosions, although three at once might be a problem

Critical hits from arrows are easy to pull off – just deliver a fully drawn shot!

CRITICAL HITS

Critical hits deal up to 50% more damage than a regular attack plus one extra point, and are recognisable by the 'star' effect seen when they strike (or, in the case of arrows, are released). Critical hits can be performed on any entity that takes damage, including players, mobs, vehicles and paintings.

For melee attacks, a critical hit occurs if the player strikes while falling down (i.e. dropping off a block or on the landing of a jump). For bows, they occur when a fully charged arrow is released. Mastering critical attacks will help you kill weaker foes much quicker – a critical attack from a diamond sword can deal as much as 12 damage, allowing you to kill many enemies in two hits.

MOB INVINCIBILITY

After mobs take damage, they'll remain invincible for a second or so after they turn red. During this time, they can't take any damage. This mechanism means that it makes more sense, in a fight, to rapidly switch between enemies rather than constantly attack the same one. In this manner, you can guarantee every landing attack will have an effect, speeding up fights.

BUNNY HOPPING

Bunny hopping describes the technique of moving around whilst continually jumping, and is useful for multiple reasons. As well as confusing the aim of attacking enemies, it allows faster mobility than running alone (jumps travel more ground than sprinting for the same amount of time will) and greatly increases the chance you have of perform a critical hit, because you spend more time in the air. There's no specific penalty for this, although it will make it harder for you to aim your own attacks and is useful for escaping large groups of foes if a fight becomes overwhelming.

KNOCKBACKS

If you strike a foe while sprinting, the enemy will incur 'knockback', which pushes them away from you by a certain number of blocks. This can be used offensively, to knock mobs off large drops or into lava, or defensively, preventing enemies from retaliating after you've attacked. It's particularly useful for creepers, allowing you a greater chance to retreat before they explode! Weapon knockback can also be increased by using enchantments and, although the player is vulnerable to it, there are enchantments that can reduce its effect (i.e. the Blast Protection armour enchantment).

Time to sit back and relax whilst your food comes to you

As the saying goes: give a person a fish and you feed them for a day. But teach them how to fish, and they can feed for a lifetime. It's time to learn yourself a trade.

Fishing in Minecraft is a great technique for gathering food, and one that's often overlooked in favour of slaughtering the animals that roam grasslands and forests. The problem with this is that animals don't respawn once you kill them, and if you don't farm the landscape will soon be barren.

Water, on the other hand, hides an abundance of fishy treats. In stark contrast to real life, it offers a never-ending supply with no quotas and no tariffs. And, best of all, every fish is line-caught. Here's how you do it...

GONE FISHIN': THE ANGLER'S GUIDEBOOK

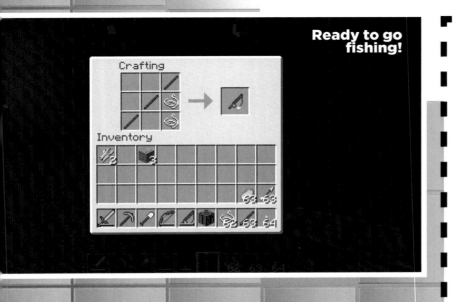

Ready to go fishing!

STEP 1: GET A FISHING ROD

Fishing rods aren't difficult to make – all you need are sticks and string. Sticks can be crafted from any available wood, while string is primarily acquired by killing spiders and/or harvesting spider webs underground. A new, unused fishing rod will have 65 durability, meaning it can be reeled in 65 times before it breaks, giving you that many chances to catch yourself an ocean-fresh meal.

STEP 2: FIND A NICE, QUIET SPOT

As in real life, fishing is best conducted away from the distractions of the world. In the real world, that might mean switching off your mobile phone, but in Minecraft it means somewhere that you won't be attacked by zombies. It's entirely possible to fish underground, or at night, but it's a distinctly unrelaxing process. In truth, you can fish in any body of water, but the more scenic, the better. You're going to spend a long time looking at this view...

You can fish anywhere, even in tiny pools like this

STEP 3: CAST AWAY

When you've cast your line into the water, you'll see the bobber land and begin to float. Now play the waiting game. You'll eventually see bubbles and disturbance on the surface, followed by a splash as it dips far below the water. When this happens, reel your line in! You've had a bite, and there's about a half-second window of opportunity before your prize gets away. If successful, the fish will fly through the air towards you. If you cast the line close enough (and your inventory isn't full), it will land in your pocket, otherwise you may have to wade out to get it. Long casts can cause the fish to fly over your head, so stand near a tree or cliff to block it. You can fish from boats, but there's more chance of missing your catch.

ROD THE IMPALER

The fishing rod can be used to attack mobs, both hostile and non-hostile. If you hit a mob when casting, you can reel them towards you. This causes no harm, but can be used to cause fall damage, pull a mob into lava, or to put them within easy melee range. Alternatively, you can use the fishing rod to hook minecarts and boats, although this does have a chance of breaking the vehicle in question.

STEP 4: RINSE, REPEAT

Fishing for long periods may become boring, but at least you can work on refining your technique.

You can move around while you've cast your line, but if you walk more than 35 blocks' distance from the bobber it will disappear automatically. The rod will suffer more damage if the hook hits a block, so try not to miss the water when you cast. And remember that there's a knack to catching a fish. Fishing outdoors when it's raining gives you a 40% better chance of catching a fish. On average, you can expect one every 15 seconds, while fishing indoors or in normal water gives you a chance of catching one every 25 seconds.

Reeling in your catch adds it directly to your inventory, if you grab it

Fishing from a boat is a safe way to do so whilst avoiding mobs

TEMPLES

Minecraft features a few randomly generated structures, including strongholds, villages and trap-filled temples. The latter of these come, as you might expect, with real dangers.

There are three types of temple – desert, jungle and ocean – and each has its own perils and pitfalls. They house hidden chests that contain random goodies. Sometimes these chests can be useful, but not always. Often they're a source of emeralds and even horse armour, making exploration worthwhile. In order to reach the potential treasure a temple holds, you'll have to solve puzzles and overcome traps, but this isn't as difficult as you may think.

DESERT TEMPLES

Desert temples look like pyramids with towers perched in front. You can find them whilst wandering the world, and can bump into them whilst mining in a desert biome. If you hit a very tall structure of sandstone, it's probable you'll find a temple if you dig back up.

The temple's interior is fairly simple and contains

Desert temples hold some great loot, if you can survive them

three levels: a topmost interior balcony, a main central chamber with exits to the towers, and a secret, hidden chamber below where you'll find the loot.

In the main chamber, you'll see an orange and blue wool pattern on the floor. The blue wool and immediate surrounding blocks hide a deep pit, at the bottom of which are four chests. There's also a pressure plate in the middle. This plate will detonate nine blocks of TNT, killing you and destroying the loot.

Take care not to step on the plate. You can use many methods, such as digging down and into the chamber and destroying the plate. Or build ladders down. An easy way is to break a corner block, and pour a bucket of water down to the bottom, riding the current to safety before destroying the pressure plate. Whichever way you choose, you can then help yourself to the chests, which will contain random but usually valuable items, including emeralds, iron ingots, gold ingots, enchanted books, saddles, horse armour, rotten flesh and bones. Don't forget to grab the TNT too, which can be found under the chest room floor. It's the only place you'll find naturally occurring TNT, and nine blocks of it for free is an offer too good to pass up.

The main chamber hides the treasure beneath

JUNGLE TEMPLES

Jungle temples are moss- and vine-covered structures that again contain three floors. The top floor contains nothing of interest, but the ground floor and basement hold secrets.

If you wander down the steps, you'll find three levers and, further around, the corridor leads to a large room with a chest. The corridor and chest room hold traps, with tripwire-activated arrow dispensers. The dispensers are hidden by vines and are easily avoided. You can disarm the tripwire with shears if you have them.

The three levers back near the stairs, if pulled in the right order, open a door in the floor next to the stairs you first came down back in the main entry hall. There's another chest there. The solution changes depending on which side of the stairs the levers are on. If the stairs are to the left, pull the levers in the order, right, left, left, right. If they're on the right, pull left, right, right, left. If you have trouble, you can simply break your way through with a pickaxe.

Jungle temples may not be as well endowed when it comes to offering decent riches, but they're the only places in the game where you can find naturally occurring chiselled stone, sticky pistons and redstone circuitry. So, even if you're not all that happy with the contents of the chests, you can grab these materials. You can also grab any unspent arrows from the dispensers.

Jungle temples can be hard to spot in the dense jungle landscape

The lever puzzle is simple enough and, if you can't do it, you can always dig

OCEAN MONUMENTS

Ocean monuments are rare and appear only in deep ocean biomes. They're the largest of the temples, and are protected by guardians and elder guardians. You'll find a ton of prismarine, which the temple is made of, as well as eight gold blocks in the treasure room too.

The difficulty here, aside from the guardians, is the underwater nature of the monument. Bring plenty of potions of water breathing and a good, preferably diamond, sword.

The easiest way to get to the gold is to dig right into the wall as you swim into the main entrance. This will bypass the randomly generated maze and make getting the gold easy. To make it easier to actually find an ocean monument, use potions of night vision. This lets you see into the water from above, and better when submerged.

Ocean monuments are huge, dangerous structures

MINECRAFT:

If you've made it this far, you must be doing something right, as this is the part of the guide that's all about the really advanced tips, advice and help that the truly experienced players want to know! That's not to say that there aren't things in here that others will find useful, it's just that we've targeted this chapter at the most experienced of Minecraft players.

So what kind of things are we going to be talking about? Well, as you can see from the list over on the right-hand page, it's a lot of the things that you might not even think about when you first start playing the game.

Take the Winning Minecraft pages. Even though Minecraft is technically an open-world game, as you make your way through it more and more it does start to become clear that there's a finale of sorts in sight. We're not going to tell you what it is here – there are marked spoilers in the piece itself – but it's one example of the treats that await you as you get heavily into the game. Do be warned: what we're going to be talking about is far from easy!

Even before you get that far though, there's one of the most dangerous places in the game: the Nether. That alone takes some work to get through! One tip: we're talking about things that take place near the end of the game, so don't spoil it for yourself. Part of the fun is discovering things for yourself when you encounter them!

84-87 **CIRCUITS**

88-91 **NETHER PORTALS**

92-95 **THE NETHER**

96-99 **ENCHANTMENTS**

100-103 **POTION BREWING**

104-105 **BEACONS**

106-109 **WINNING MINECRAFT: THE END**

110-111 **WINNING MINECRAFT: THE WITHER**

ADVANCED

REDSTONE CIRCUITS AND MECHANISMS

**Redsto[...]
wire passe[...]
charge fo[...]
blocks bef[...]
it fizzles [...]**

Circuits in Minecraft are incredibly complicated. We could probably fill an entire guide with information about circuits and their component parts alone! It's impossible to cover all of the tricks, techniques, intricacies and behaviours of Minecraft's redstone circuitry without also including a crash course in electronics and electrical logic. If that's what you were hoping for, there are probably some good books in your local library.

However, even if it's not possible to give you a crash course in the entire electronics components of Minecraft in a few pages, we can at least get you started. If you're wondering what redstone can be used for, don't worry. By the end of this section, you'll understand how circuits work, recognise some of the basic components, and be ready to take on the challenge of building your first circuits!

THE BASICS

Redstone circuits are composed using redstone wire (made by placing redstone dust on existing blocks) and redstone power supplies, such as torches. Circuits have a deep level of interactivity, and can be built to respond to player actions or to using self-generated feedback mechanisms. Plant growth, hostile mobs, friendly mobs and even ambient details such as light conditions can trigger various components of redstone circuitry. Like much of Minecraft, the main limits are the boundaries of your imagination and technical know-how!

Redstone circuits also incorporate a number of basic component types. As well as interactive components such as buttons, pressure plates and triggers, the game contains transmission components, which move power around a system (wires, repeaters and comparators) and mechanism components, such as pistons, lamps and dispensers.

Power travels through redstone circuits the same way electricity travels through a conventional circuit. Blocks can be powered or unpowered, and some blocks will change their state depending on which. Wire will glow, pistons will move, lamps will ignite, etc. The power level provided by power sources can vary between 0 and 15, and this can have effects on things like triggers and sensors.

The strength of power transmitted through redstone diminishes by one unit for each block of wire it's transmitted. After 15 blocks (at most), redstone wire will need to be strengthened by a repeater or comparator. Although signals can travel long distances, it's worth remembering that they can only affect loaded game chunks. Travel too far and the circuit will be unloaded, causing it to temporarily cease operation.

Redstone circuits operate on their own internal timing system, which updates ten times a second. Each update is known as a 'tick', and different components require different numbers of ticks to react the signal changes and propagate their effects.

REDSTONE COMPONENTS

Minecraft contains a huge number of blocks that respond to and translate redstone power signals. We can't cover them all in great detail, but to get you started here are some of the most useful!

Redstone blocks are solid blocks of redstone, created by crafting together nine units of redstone dust. They provide an always-on power source, which can be placed and moved around by pistons.

Buttons can be made of either wood or stone. When pushed, they generate a pulse of power that remains active for ten ticks (stone) or 15 ticks (wood).

Pressure plates can also be made of either wood or stone, and are triggered by entities resting on top of them. Stone plates react to mobs and players only, while wooden ones are activated by items as well. When activated, they produce power until deactivated.

Daylight sensors measure the strength of the sun, based on its position in the sky. They turn 'on' at dawn and 'off' at night. Power varies between 1 and 15, depending on how high in the sky.

Levers are used to switch circuits on or off. Unlike buttons, they'll create a constant stream of power until they're deactivated.

Redstone torches are used to transmit power to blocks, and in particular to transmit power vertically. It's possible to temporarily short out redstone torches by activating and deactivating them too quickly.

Redstone repeaters are used to retransmit power when signals become weak – normally after 15 blocks of travel through a redstone wire. Repeaters can be used to propagate power in a specific direction, as they only accept input from the rear and output to the front. It's also possible to set a repeat delay of 1-4 ticks.

Dispensers are mechanisms that interact with the environment, but have a large number of effects depending on their contents. If a dispenser contains armour, for example, it will equip the armour to any player within a one-block distance when it's activated. If the dispenser contains an arrow, it will fire a weak arrow in the direction it's facing. Bone meal will increment the growth of any adjacent plants. There are other special effects, but for the majority of blocks the dispenser will simply drop a block of the type contained within it – literally 'dispensing' a block.

Doors can be made of wood or iron. Although wooden doors can be opened manually, as well as by redstone circuits, iron doors can only be opened and closed by powered redstone components (such as an adjacent button).

Fence gates act like wooden doors, except that they resemble sections of fence and close automatically if a block update is detected nearby. Trapdoors are similarly activated and deactivated by redstone, although they have the added effect of allowing any items, mobs or players resting on top of them to fall when they open.

Droppers will cause a random item from an adjacent object's inventory to be dropped, as if from a player's inventory. They can face in any direction, and if they're facing another container they'll transfer the item into it. Long chains of droppers can be used to transfer items over long distances quickly. Droppers transfer items one block per tick, so an item can travel through ten droppers in one second.

Hoppers are used to collect dropped items and channel them in any direction. Unlike droppers, they don't automatically dispense the item they contain. Rather, they push their current item out, replacing it with the new item. This occurs every four ticks as long as the block is powered.

Note blocks are used to create sounds when powered or hit. The sound a note block makes is determined by the block placed beneath it. Note blocks won't work if there's a block placed directly above them!

Pistons come in two types: regular and sticky. Pistons push blocks, while sticky pistons can both push and pull them. When activated, a piston can push any blocks placed in front of it between 1 and 12 blocks' distance. When deactivated, the piston arm will retract, leaving the block in place (or, in the case of sticky pistons, withdrawing it as well). Pistons can also be used to manipulate mobs and items. Block behaviour isn't consistent, however – some blocks can't be pushed at all, while others will be destroyed by a piston interaction.

Redstone lamps provide light. They're immediately activated by power, but take two ticks to deactivate when power is removed. Redstone lamp light is set at level 15, one higher than torches, making them good for lighting an area or creating automated growing systems.

TNT is used to create an explosion. When activated, the TNT will become primed and explode after 40 ticks, destroying blocks within its blast radius.

BUILDING TIPS

When building a circuit, there are a number of conditions that should be kept in mind to ensure optimal conditions for running.

As in real life, redstone circuits interact poorly with water. Water will cause redstone wire to pop away from the block it's resting on, rendering the circuit useless. If the circuit is built in a vulnerable location, it may be a good idea to encase it completely (you can use glass blocks if you want to keep the wires visible!).

When building circuits, many people find it useful to lay wires on only a specific, uncommon type of block, such as wool, snow or bricks. This makes it easy to identify blocks that are covered in circuits from multiple angles, meaning you're unlikely to accidentally damage a circuit while mining.

When building circuits with explosive components, don't ever place the TNT until the circuit has been fully tested! A misplaced power source or wire could cause the TNT to explode, causing significant damage to the surrounding circuitry. Always use some other indicator in place of the explosive parts until the very last moment!

Minecarts and rails can also be integrated into redstone systems. See the section on minecarts and rails for more details about the options available! Boats can also be used as part of redstone systems due to their behaviour, but there are no special properties involved – they can simply be pushed across water to activate triggers or interact with mechanisms when they come into contact with them.

NETHER PORTALS

As you get further into the game, you'll discover that Minecraft hides a terrifying secret. One that might actually explain where all these weird monsters and stuff are coming from. You see, there's a parallel world out there called the Nether – a hell-like dimension filled with enemies and horror. You don't have to go there, but if you want to – and what explorer wouldn't? – there's only one way to do so: you have to build your own portal.

Portals are the gateways between the Overworld (the verdant green lands you play most of the game in) and the Nether. If you want to beat the game, you'll have to get used to using them, but they also have other properties that might be interesting to advanced Minecrafters. In this section of the guide, we'll teach you all about portals: how to build them, how to use them, why you would want to use them, and why they're so important to the game.

PART 1:
BUILDING A NETHER PORTAL

Building a Nether portal isn't actually that difficult. It's getting to the point where you've got the tools you need to build one that takes the most time!

To create a Nether portal, you need two things: ten or 14 blocks of obsidian and a flint and steel with which to ignite the portal once it's built. To get the raw materials, you must also have obtained enough diamond to build a diamond pickaxe, which then allows you to mine obsidian. Although it's possible to shortcut your way there, it's safe to say most players won't be visiting the Nether very early on in their Minecraft experience!

The crucial component of a portal – the obsidian needed for its frame – is reasonably rare in its naturally occurring state. Unlike almost every other type of block, obsidian doesn't spawn when the map chunks are generated. Instead, it's created by a simple but accidental combination of water and lava, meaning

that any obsidian you encounter in the Overworld has been generated by coincidence, rather than through seeded randomness like most blocks are. Luckily, obsidian is also quite easy to manufacture artificially, so if you haven't managed to find any you can, at the very least, create your own without too much effort.

Specifically, lava is transformed into obsidian when flowing water hits it, meaning that obsidian blocks are most frequently found in deep caverns where underground springs flow onto lava lakes. Blocks where flowing water meets flowing lava will turn into cobblestone rather than obsidian. The good news is that the way it's created means that once you find obsidian, you're likely to find a lot of it in one go.

The bad news is that there's no guarantee you'll find any.

Mining obsidian also takes a long time, at least compared to any other block. It takes almost ten seconds to mine each piece when using an unenchanted diamond pickaxe (dropping to a minimum of 2.55 seconds with a pickaxe enchanted with Efficiency V). It's possible to destroy obsidian blocks with other tools, but not to mine them – and it takes more than four minutes to destroy a single piece!

Mining obsidian is also potentially dangerous – by its nature, it's often sitting atop deep lava – so creating an obsidian farm is the smartest and most reliable way to get what you need for your portal. Simply create a 2x5 trench and fill it with lava, which can be easily obtained without venturing too far below ground. You'll need ten blocks of lava in all to make sure that the trench is full and that the lava isn't flowing in any direction. Surround the pool with dirt or cobblestone (just to stop the water going everywhere!) and place a water source block on top of the lava. The lava will turn into obsidian. Remove the water source block and you'll be free to mine your newly created blocks.

...during...

An obsidian farm before...

Once you've collected the obsidian, you now have to build a portal frame, which requires 14 blocks of obsidian, but you can leave out the corners and get away with only ten blocks if you prefer. Once the frame is complete, you must ignite the portal to activate it. This can be done most simply by using a flint and steel to set a small fire within the boundaries. If everything has gone correctly, the portal will become active and the interior of the frame will show the purple 'portal' effect. It will also create an associated exit portal in the Nether. Remaining inside an active portal frame for four seconds will take you between the two worlds.

Portals are quite resistant to damage because of their obsidian frames, and because the portal itself can't be manually removed. Explosions can destroy portal blocks, which will deactivate the entire portal, although it can be simply re-ignited. To destroy a portal completely, you must remove one of the ten non-optional blocks from the frame (i.e. not one of the corner blocks). This will render the portal inoperable until the frame is repaired.

You can also create a portal without the diamond pickaxe by 'casting' lava into obsidian in the correct shape, then igniting it.

PART 2:
USING PORTALS

Although initially responsive to players only, in current versions of Minecraft portals can be used by almost any entity. Mobs (hostile and peaceful) will travel to the Nether if they enter the portal, as will thrown items and vehicles. Notably, vehicles with passengers can't currently travel to and from the Nether using a portal, meaning that freight can travel inter-dimensionally, but passengers can't.

Beware that building a portal in the Overworld will cause zombie pigmen to occasionally spawn near it unless the difficulty is set to Peaceful. Don't build a portal near to your home or base unless you're looking for a fight!

Although the primary use for portals is travelling to the Nether, they can be used for another purpose: fast travelling through the Overworld via the Nether.

In the Nether, one block's distance corresponds to eight in the Overworld (three in the console versions), but on the X and Z axis only. Height on the Y axis is taken into account, but matches the Overworld as

...and after!

A portal in the Nether, set up for fast travelling. Please keep your hands inside the dimensional rift!

closely as possible. By travelling through the Nether and creating an exit portal, you can cross great distances in the Overworld in a relatively short period of time, which is useful for exploring, although, obviously, there's a significant risk involved in crossing the Nether. Bring weapons and armour!

If you create a portal in the Nether, then use it, the game will automatically create a corresponding exit portal in the Overworld. Remember that to do this, you'll have to bring the materials you need into the Nether with you – there's no naturally occurring obsidian in the Nether and water will evaporate the moment it's dropped.

When exit portals are created (in the Overworld or Nether), they'll pick the nearest viable location to spawn, which means it's possible for them to appear in unusual locations – on top of trees, or deep underground – but never in places that would be inaccessible or dangerous (i.e. underwater or inside bedrock). The search radius for generating exit portals is 16 blocks in any direction on the X and Z axis, and although the orientation is matched if possible, the game will spawn portals facing in different directions if there's no viable alternative. If there's absolutely no place to safely spawn a portal, the game will force the creation of one in the first piece of available space, with four blocks of obsidian either side to act as a platform above potentially dangerous terrain.

Beware that portals which are generated within a 128-block radius of an existing portal in the Nether (or a 1,024-block radius in the Overworld) will likely connect to the same exit portal, which can potentially create confusing relationships, where players can enter different portals but reach the same exit, or be unable to return to an existing portal. If this happens, you can dismantle a portal and move it without affecting the relationships of existing portals, which are calculated each time a portal is used rather than being fixed at the time of creation.

Remember that despite the Nether's hostile environment, the construction of a portal and proper use of the Nether is a necessary step towards Minecraft's end game, as well as a source of convenient items and fast travel.

An economical ten-block portal

Once you successfully harvest enough obsidian and build a portal to it, you'll eventually find yourself in the Nether, the reason for all your hard work so far. However, the Nether isn't going to reward you for your efforts with a celebratory fanfare or arrival party, oh no. Instead, you'll be plunged into a hellish world full of fire, lava, treacherous caves and deadly enemies.

It's certainly no picnic, and you may ask yourself what you're actually doing here. Why not just go back to the relative safety of the Overworld? Well, because as dangerous as it is, the Nether holds a host of rare and essential materials that you'll need it you want to craft some of the game's rarer and most powerful items. And, if you intend to face the ender dragon, you're going to need some of these. So, take a deep breath, grip that trusty sword and step boldly forward.

WHAT IS THE NETHER?

The Nether is an evil alternate dimension that you travel to using a Nether portal. Like the Overworld, it stretches out infinitely (on the PC anyway; the console is limited like its version of the Overworld). It has a finite depth, however, and both the top- and bottom-most layers are made of indestructible bedrock. There's no day or night in the Nether, and only pits of lava, sporadic clusters of glowstone and instances of fire provide any illumination.

Welcome to the Nether, where the weather's always scorching and the residents are eager to meet and eat you

Many resources can be found in the Nether, but it's dangerous work finding them

It's a dangerous place, filled with nasty creatures, lava and the constant threat of death, but to succeed in Minecraft you'll have to face the Nether

THE NETHER

Much of the Nether is made up of Netherrack, which forms the majority of the world's craggy and perilous cliffs. Narrow corridors snake through the mostly open, cavernous landscape, which is filled with an endless ocean of lava.

It's a very barren place, punctuated by Nether fortresses. These are naturally spawning structures made of Nether brick, and they house many of the Nether's dangerous foes, including monster spawners. It's in these fortresses that you'll find much of the Nether's most valuable materials. Unfortunately, to grab these items, you'll need to do battle with the dangerous creatures that lay in wait within. Fortresses are also a source of Nether wart, which you'll find growing in soul sand inside. You can also harvest the Nether brick, stairs and fencing easily enough.

Glowstone provides some of the Nether's only light, and can be harvested, but you'll need to climb

Outside of the fortresses spawn armies of zombie pigmen and ghasts, and you can find glowstone deposits hanging from cave ceilings, and soul sand spread around areas of the ground. Nether quartz can also be found, along with mushrooms.

PREPARING FOR THE NETHER

Before you even think about stepping through your Nether portal, there are a few preparations you should make

if you're going to succeed in your excursion. If you don't, you'll find the Nether far more difficult than it needs to be.

First, make sure your attack and defence are up to scratch. The better the equipment you have, the better your chances. At least ensure you have some armour and a decent, preferably enchanted, sword. A bow and plenty of arrows are essential – don't even think of going to the Nether without them.

Much of the Nether's environmental hazards and enemy attacks are fire based, so if you have any golden or enchanted apples they'll be very useful. Any form of fire resistance you can muster is highly advised. Fire resistance potions are ideal, but until you visit the Nether to find and kill a blaze to grab a blaze rod you won't be able to brew them. You may have some if you've been lucky enough to grab them from fallen witches in the Overworld, though. If so, bring 'em along.

One of the most important supplies you'll need are torches. The Nether is a very dark place, with little natural light, so you'll need to make your own. If you don't, you'll find exploring the Nether almost impossible.

Other equipment you'll need includes a few pickaxes for mining, spades for digging up soul sand and, if you want to stock up on lava, some buckets. However, due to the risky nature of the Nether, it's advisable to leave valuable items and tools at home, such as diamond equipment. If you die in the Nether, you'll respawn in the Overworld and, unless you're quick or very lucky, getting your dropped items back can be very difficult. Iron pickaxes and other tools are perfectly fine for mining Netherrack and other resources, so you don't need better tools here anyway.

If you have one, it's a good idea to bring an empty map. This helps keep your bearings, as the Nether is far more disorienting than anywhere in the Overworld, and it's easy to lose track of your entry portal if you're not careful.

THINGS TO DO IN THE NETHER

The Nether isn't exactly a place you'll want to set up home, but frequent visits will be needed to harvest rare materials. The most basic trip to the Nether can be to gather easy-to-mine Netherrack and soul sand. Netherrack is useful for building certain items, such as defensive fire pits (see the Defending your home chapter), but as it's easy to set on fire and burns forever it's not all that useful for much else, save for decoration. Glowstones and glowdust can be found too, but it's always stuck to ceilings, making it hard to reach.

Soul sand slows down anything that crosses it, also making it useful for defence, and it's the only block that will grow Nether wart. Both blocks are useful and can be found in abundance, along with mushrooms. Look around the

landscape enough and you'll also find Nether quartz in tunnels and caves.

Enemies roaming the caves can be farmed for useful stuff too. Zombie pigmen can be harvested for rotten flesh, gold nuggets, and rarely gold ingots and swords. They're friendly until you attack them, and if attacked they won't only retaliate, but any pigmen in the vicinity will also attack. You can quickly become overwhelmed, so be prepared. Build a safe structure to hide in, or pick them off when they're alone for best results.

Nether fortresses are bleak citadels of pain, and house essential resources

Ghasts are large, flying creatures that shoot explosive fireballs. These do plenty of damage and also set fire to any Netherrack in the vicinity, adding to the difficulty. Luckily, ghasts can be killed with 2-3 arrows, and are large enough to hit easily. You can also deflect their fireballs back at them by hitting them with melee attacks or an arrow, but this is tricky and requires careful timing. When killed, they may drop a ghast tear. This can be hard to obtain as ghasts often fly over lava, so be sure to kill them over land if you can.

Although these resources can be useful, it's Nether fortresses you'll want to find. A great source of Nether brick, much of the bounty is to be found here. Nether wart grows exclusively in fortresses, so keep an eye out for this, as it's used in potion brewing.

Ghasts are dangerous and can see you from a very long distance away

The main focus in fortresses is on enemies, in particular blazes and magma cubes. Let's look at blazes first.

Blazes are, arguably, the Nether's most dangerous enemy. They're found only in fortresses and can quickly kill you with a volley of fireballs. They can fly and are often encountered next to monster spawners, making them far more dangerous due to sheer weight of numbers. Despite the danger, though, you have to kill them, as they can drop blaze rods, used to make potion brewing stands.

To do this, it's best to use arrows from a distance, using any cover to protect yourself. Even if you're very careful, you'll probably get hit, and so you'll need to heal up. It's here fire resistance comes in very handy, so if you have any use it. Armour is all but useless here due to the fire damage.

Snowballs also work against blazes, so bring some along, as it makes it easier to get up close to them and finish them with your sword. Just be careful not to kill them over a large pit or above lava, as anything they drop, including blaze rods, will be lost. If you intend to farm blazes, don't destroy the monster spawner.

Iron golems can be useful when fighting blazes, so if you can build one, it's a good idea, even if you only use it for cover.

Magma cubes are another important enemy, as they drop magma cream. They're easier to kill than blazes

and behave in the same way as Overworld slimes, splitting into smaller cubes when hit. So, break them down with arrows and, when small enough, finish them off with your sword.

Wither skeletons are dangerous versions of normal skeletons and are armed

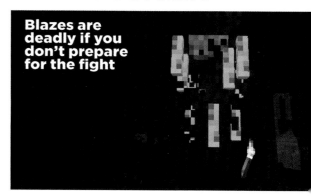

Blazes are deadly if you don't prepare for the fight

with stone swords. If they hit you, they can cause the status effect, wither. This is like poison, but can also kill you (poison won't drop your health lower than half a heart). They hit harder and are tougher. When killed, they can drop wither skulls. These are used to summon the wither boss, so if you want to fight it you'll need to kill some wither skeletons.

Killing them is easy enough if you're prepared. Simply use arrows, or hit them with your sword, back off, then repeat. If you're hit and suffer from wither, simply retreat and heal up. They very rarely drop wither skulls, so you may have to do a lot of skeleton hunting to gather the three required to summon the wither.

An anvil waiting for the hammer to fall

nce you've exhausted the limits that physical laws place on your Minecraft experience, don't make the mistake of thinking that there's nothing left to find. Come with us now as we enter a world of magic and sorcery, or, as Minecraft calls it, enchanting.

CAST A SPELL

Although it's possible to find pre-enchanted items in Minecraft (recognisable by their purple glow) in chests and, occasionally, as mob drops, a more reliable way of getting them is to simply have your existing tools and items enchanted. There are three ways in which you can do this. The first is to use an enchantment table to apply your own enchantments. Doing so will require you to spend experience points, but also has the advantage of giving you fine control over what spell is cast and how strong it is.

The second is to use an anvil. You can use anvils to combine a normal tool with an enchanted version, or to combine an enchanted book with any existing item to transfer its spell. Again, this costs experience points, but can be an effective way to 'repair' enchanted items, since if you repair enchanted items normally (using a crafting table) the enchantment will be lost.

The final and arguably least convenient way to apply an enchantment is to buy enchantments for your items in

exchange for emeralds from villagers. Priests can no longer add enchantments to items as they could before version 1.8 and sell enchantment books instead. Librarians sell these books, and clerics sell bottles 'o' enchanting. Other villagers, such as weapon and toolsmiths, now sell pre-enchanted items.

ENCHAN

Enchanted pickaxes can mine materials you usually wouldn't be able to grab

Repair & Name

Diamond Pickaxe

Diamo
Silk T

Enchantment Cost

+5 At

ENCHANTMENT TABLES & ANVILS

Enchantment tables are created using a mixture of diamonds, obsidian blocks and a book, and are used to directly enchant items. To enchant an item, simply place it on top of the table (similar to the way you'd use a crafting table), along with some lapis lazuli, and select the spell you want to enchant it with, spending your experience in the process.

Note that the enchantments an

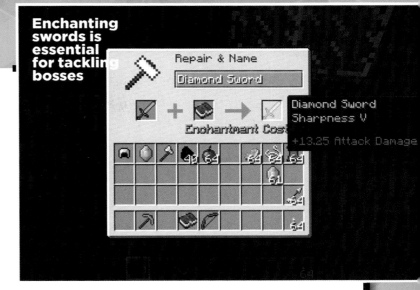

Enchanting swords is essential for tackling bosses

cost more experience to cast, but have a greater chance of producing a higher-level enchantment, and can even apply multiple effects simultaneously (up to three).

Anvils are created by combining blocks of iron and iron ingots, and are used expressly for combining the enchantment statuses of two items (and, in the case of two similar items, their durability). To combine items, place the item you want to improve in the first slot and the item you want to destroy in the second slot. If the items can be combined, the enchanted item will appear in the output slot alongside a number that indicates the experience cost of forging it. Removing the item from the output slot spends your experience points and allows you to add the item to your inventory.

By using the anvil to combine an item with an enchanted book, you can apply the specific enchantment without the risk of choosing a weak or incorrect spell. If you've got an item with an enchantment you don't want to lose, this will enable you to continue using it without any risk of

item accepts are determined by various factors. The material an item is made of does have some influence – gold enchants more readily, meaning spells tend to be stronger. Some items can't be enchanted on an enchanting table at all (for example, the hoe and shears) but will accept enchantments from an anvil.

Initially, enchantment tables will only apply low-level spells, but you can increase the power of their enchantments by surrounding them with bookshelves, leaving a one-block gap between them and the enchantment tables. When placed correctly, arcane glyphs will be drawn from the books into the table, indicating their effects. Stronger spells

losing it! You can also use the anvil to give items a new name, although this will cost an experience surcharge!

ENCHANTMENT MATHS

The enchantment process contains a strong element of randomness, however it's possible to guide it towards certain effects, if not directly influence the outcome with complete certainty. The first 16 levels of enchantment are the 'cheapest' because each of those experience levels requires the same amount of experience points to reach. Beyond that, levelling is harder, with each experience level requiring more experience points to reach than the last.

One of the difficulties encountered when enchanting items is that the spell options are presented in a coded language. The names have no clear meaning, so be sure to roll over each spell to find out its English name, instead of hoping for a good enchantment!

It may make more sense to enchant books than items, since you can then use an anvil to combine the book with an appropriate item.

That said, books can only hold one enchantment at a time, so the gamble of directly enchanting an item may hold more appeal. Nonetheless, books can be used to add enchantments to items that would

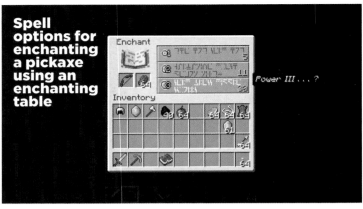

Spell options for enchanting a pickaxe using an enchanting table

otherwise be unable to receive them – for example, to add the Unbreaking enchantment to a sword.

The strongest enchantments require 30 experience levels to cast, but beware that there's no guarantee that high-level enchanting will yield the highest-level enchantments possible, or more than one enchantment! You could still end up with a level two or three spell, and may only receive one effect rather than multiple effects.

When using an anvil, the cost of forging depends on various factors, including the strength of the enchantments applied and the rarity of the material used in the item (i.e. diamond tools require more experience to forge with than iron tools). Items that have been forged multiple times have a greater experience cost, but you can circumvent this by changing the name each time, tricking the game into treating each enchantment as a new one!

Surround your enchanting table with bookshelves to increase the power of your enchantments

LIST OF ENCHANTMENTS

ID	Name	Effect
		ARMOUR ENCHANTMENTS
0	Protection	Reduces damage
1	Fire Protection	Resists fire damage, reduces burn time
2	Feather Falling	Reduces fall damage
3	Blast Protection	Reduces explosion damage and knockback
4	Projectile Protection	Reduces projectile damage
5	Respiration	Improves underwater breathing time and vision, reduces drowning damage
6	Aqua Affinity	Improves underwater mining rate
7	Thorns	Attackers take damage
8	Depth Strider	Increased movement whilst underwater
		SWORD ENCHANTMENTS
16	Sharpness	Increases damage
17	Smite	Causes more damage to undead mobs
18	Bane of Arthropods	Causes more damage to insects and arachnids
19	Knockback	Increases knockback caused
20	Fire Aspect	Sets target on fire
21	Looting	Mobs drop more loot
		TOOL ENCHANTMENTS
32	Efficiency	Speeds up mining (+30% per level)
33	Silk Touch	Collect blocks in unmined form (i.e. diamond ore instead of diamond)
34	Unbreaking	Improves durability (can also be applied to armour and weapons)
35	Fortune	Increases amount of resources dropped from blocks
		BOW ENCHANTMENTS
48	Power	Increases bow damage
49	Punch	More knockback from arrows
50	Flame	Arrows deal fire damage
51	Infinity	Bow doesn't consume arrows
		FISHING ROD ENCHANTMENTS
61	Luck of the Sea	Decreases chance of finding junk
62	Lure	Increases the rate of fish biting your hook

POTION BREWING

In order to acquire potions, some of the most useful and powerful items in the game, you'll need to master potion brewing

A long with the basic ability to craft items and materials, Minecraft also lets you brew potions which can bestow a range of effects. Potions are brewed using a brewing stand and a collection of ingredients. Before you can begin brewing, though, you'll first need to acquire the basics.

You'll need a brewing stand to make potions, the cauldron is optional

BREWING PREPARATIONS

To even think of brewing a potion, you'll first need some basic equipment, chief of which is a brewing stand. These can be built via a crafting bench, but one of the materials required is harder to get than most.

A brewing stand requires three blocks of cobblestone, which are easy to get, but also requires a blaze rod. These are found by killing Blazes in The Nether (see The Nether section of this guide for more information). This is a dangerous task requiring a lot of preparation, so it'll be some time into a new game before you can get one. When you do, though, simply construct a brewing

stand using any workbench. Next you need some empty glass bottles. These are made using three blocks of glass each, and a brewing stand can hold up to three bottles at any one time.

You'll then need some water to use as a potion base. You can fill bottles from any still water source, such as a pre-built well, or a nearby body of water. You can also uild a cauldron, which can hold hough water to fill three bottles. Finally, you'll need ingredients. ome of these are easy to obtain, nd others can be very difficult. f course, the best potions quire the harder-to-acquire gredients, such is life, but if ou brew them, they can make our life much easier, especially gainst tough mobs and bosses.

REWING 101

rewing a potion is actually ery easy. All you need to do add base ingredients to the ater, followed by a secondary gredient, and a modifier. Not l are needed, but combining em produces various effects nd potion strengths and urations. To do this, simply use e brewing stand to open the rewing interface. Add bottles to e bottom three spaces and an gredient to the top, then wait. our potion will be brewed over me. Once brewed, either add your potions, or place them in ur inventory.

f you want to create splash otions, which can then be rown as weapons, simply add unpowder to a potion.

Splash potions are made by adding gunpowder

BASE INGREDIENTS

Base ingredients are essential to a potion. Nether wart is the core ingredient, used to make a base 'awkward' potion. for most of the useful potions. Other base ingredients all produce potions that will create variations of the potion of weakness.

Ingredient	Makes
Fermented Spider Eye	Potion of Weakness
Glowstone Dust	Thick Potion
Nether Wart	Awkward Potion
Redstone	Mundane Potion

SECONDARY INGREDIENTS

Bestow an awkward potion with effects. Added to water creates a mundane potion. The exception is the fermented spider eye, which creates weakness, and golden carrots, which can't be added to water.

Ingredient	Effect
Blaze Powder	Strength
Fermented Spider Eye	Weakness
Ghast Tear	Regeneration
Glistering Melon	Instant Health
Golden Carrot	Night Vision
Magma Cream	Fire Resistance
Spider Eye	Poison
Sugar	Speed

MODIFIERS

These ingredients change the properties of a potion rather than the effects. They can change the strength and duration of a potion's core effects, making them more effective.

Ingredient	Effect
Fermented Spider Eye	Changes the basic effect and reverses it, causing a negative effect. It can also create a potion of invisibility.
Glowstone Dust	Potency increase
Gunpowder	Creates throwable 'splash' potion
Redstone	Duration increase

REVERSION

Reversion is the process of taking an existing potion and effectively weakening the effect, reverting it to the previous tier. For example, adding glowstone dust to an extended fire resistance potion (8:00 duration) will turn the potion into a reverted fire resistance potion, which has the same duration as a normal fire resistance potion (3:00 duration).

You can revert potions with three main ingredients – glowstone dust, redstone and fermented spider eyes.

POTIONS

New Potion	Base Potion Type	Ingredient	Potion Effect	Duration (minutes)
Potion of Healing	Awkward Potion	Glistering Melon	Restores 2 hearts	Instant
Potion of Fire Resistance	Awkward Potion	Magma Cream	Immunity to fire, lava, ranged Blaze attacks.	3:00
Potion of Regeneration	Awkward Potion	Ghast Tear	Health regenerates by 1 heart every 2.4 seconds.	0:45
Potion of Strength	Awkward Potion	Blaze Powder	Enhances attack power by 1 _ hearts.	3:00
Potion of Swiftness	Awkward Potion	Sugar	Speed boost, approx 20%	3:00
Potion of Night Vision	Awkward Potion	Golden Carrot	Bestows night vision, even underwater	3:00
Potion of Poison	Awkward Potion	Spider Eye	Causes poison, draining every 1.5 seconds.	0:45
Potion of Weakness	Awkward, Mundane or Thick Potion	Fermented Spider Eye	Weakens all melee attacks by 1 heart.	1:30
Potion of Weakness (extended)	Mundane Potion (extended)	Fermented Spider Eye	Weakens all melee attacks by 1 heart.	4:00
Potion of Fire Resistance (extended)	Potion of Fire Resistance (normal/ reverted)	Redstone	Immunity to fire, lava and Blaze ranging attacks	8.00
Potion of Healing II	Potion of Healing (normal/reverted)	Glowstone Dust	Restores 4 hearts	Instant
Potion of Regeneration (extended)	Potion of Regeneration I or II	Redstone	Restores 1 heart every 2.4 seconds	2.00
Potion of Regeneration II	Potion of Regeneration (normal/extended)	Glowstone Dust	Restores 1 heart every 2.4 seconds	0.16

New Potion	Base Potion Type	Ingredient	Potion Effect	Duration (minutes)
Potion of Strength (extended)	Potion of Strength I or II	Redstone	Adds 1 heart of damage to melee attacks.	8:00
Potion of Strength II	Potion of Strength (normal/extended)	Glowstone Dust	Adds 3 hearts of damage to melee attacks.	1:30
Potion of Swiftness (extended)	Potions of Swiftness (normal/ extended)	Redstone	Speed boost of approx 20%.	8:00
Potion of Swiftness II	Potions of Swiftness (normal/ extended)	Glowstone Dust	Speed boost of approx 40%.	1:30
Potion of Night Vision (extended)	Potion of Night Vision	Redstone	Night Vision	8:00
Potion of Invisibility	Potion of Night Vision	Fermented Spider Eye	Makes player (not equipment) invisible.	3:00
Potion of Invisibility (extended)	Potion of Night Vision (extended)	Fermented Spider Eye	Makes player (not equipment) invisible.	8:00
Potion of Invisibility (extended)	Potion of Invisibility	Redstone	Makes player (not equipment) invisible.	8:00

ENHANCED POTIONS

These potions are created by adding a modifier ingredient to the basic brewed potions.

Original Potion	Reverted Potions	Ingredient
Potion of Healing (reverted) or Poison (extended)	Potion of Harming (reverted)	Fermented Spider Eye
Potion of Fire Resistance (reverted) or Swiftness II	Potion of Slowness (reverted)	Fermented Spider Eye
Potion of Strength II or Regeneration II	Potion of Weakness (reverted)	Fermented Spider Eye
Potion of Fire Resistance (extended)	Potion of Fire Resistance (reverted)	Glowstone Dust
Potion of Slowness (extended)	Potion of Slowness (reverted)	Glowstone Dust
Potion of Weakness (extended)	Potion of Weakness (reverted)	Glowstone Dust
Potion of Healing II	Potion of Healing (reverted)	Redstone
Potion of Harming II	Potion of Harming (reverted)	Redstone

So, you've managed to construct and beat the much-feared wither, have you? You've beaten one of the most powerful enemies in the game, and what do you have to show for it? Probably a few bruises and spent potion bottles, as well as the only item the wither drops, a Nether star.

Nether stars look nice, all sparkly and glowing, but what good are they? Why did you just spend all that time fighting a tough-as-old-leather boss? At the moment, there's one reward-based reason worth the effort, and that's to make beacons.

Beacons are special structures you can create that serve two functions. First, they act as a guiding light to denote an important place in the game world, such as your home or a particularly rich mine.

Second, they can be used to bestow a range of status buffs to all players nearby, such as increased strength, speed and health regeneration. Very nice.

Sadly, beacons can be very costly to make, requiring a lot of metal ore or gems, and the key component of a single beacon is a Nether star. So, if you plan to make multiple beacons, you'd better be ready to create and kill multiple withers.

BEACONS

Keep losing you way, or forgetting where your house is after a bit of exploring? What you need is a beacon

Beacons are used for navigation and to grant status buffs to nearby players

BEACON CONSTRUCTION

The first step to making a beacon is to create the actual beacon block itself. To do this, you'll need a Nether star, three blocks of obsidian and five glass blocks. Once you have them, you can construct a beacon.

Once you have the beacon block, you'll then need the resources to make a base for the beacon. These bases are essentially pyramid structures made out of iron, gold, emerald or diamond bocks, with the beacon, or beacons, making the topmost level.

Now, as you can imagine, a pyramid of diamond blocks is going to be time consuming and very, very expensive. Luckily, the material a beacon's pyramid base is made of doesn't affect its power or abilities. This aspect is only affected by the actual size and configuration of the pyramid. So, if you're playing in Survival mode, you should probably stick to using iron blocks, as iron is far easier to get hold of.

Should you wish to, you can also mix these blocks together, and beacon pyramids don't have to be made out of a single type of block. So your beacon's base can be half-iron and half-gold if you like, or a chequerboard pattern of any combination. Go ahead, get creative. The most basic beacon structure is a 3x3 grid of blocks, with a beacon block on top. After a couple of seconds, a bright light will shoot up into the sky, signifying the beacon's active status.

If your beam doesn't work, then you may have issues with the location of your beacon.

For beacons to work, they have to be built with a clear view of the sky. So be sure that there are no obstructions, and that you're only using the block types listed above. Transparent blocks, such as glass, can be placed above beacons and they'll still work.

Beacons can be placed in both the Nether and the End, but ones in the Nether will only work if terrain above them is naturally generated.

If a beacon is damaged, and any blocks destroyed for any reason, it will power down. The beacon will still remember its power settings and, when rebuilt, will work again as normal.

Building larger pyramids is possible and advisable, as more levels (up to four, not including the beacon itself) makes the beacon more powerful and able to access different stat buffs and even a secondary power (see below).

You can also build pyramids large enough to feature two,

three, four or six beacons at the top. These pyramids aren't necessarily square, but can be elongated in order to accommodate the extra beacons. For example, a pyramid that holds two beacons would have a base of 10x9, making the top level two beacons in size.

BEACON POWERS

There's more to beacons than bright lights, and the major bonus they deliver is stat buffs, which are applied to any player in range. Once you build a beacon, you can use the beacon block to control the stat buffs the beacon generates.

The more levels a beacon's base has, the more powers you have available to you, and if the beacon's base is four levels high, you can also choose a secondary power as well as a primary one.

The available powers a beacon can have (depending on size) include Haste, Jump Boost, Speed, Strength and Resistance. Secondary powers include Regeneration and a Level II version of the selected primary power (only one of the secondary powers can be selected at any one time).

To activate a beacon's powers, you simply use the beacon block at the top and click the power(s) you want. Then, place either a diamond, emerald, gold ingot or iron ingot into the slot below and click the tick. The beacon will begin to emit the stat buffs.

If you build a beacon with more than one beacon block at the top, each can be set to a different power. So, as mentioned earlier, you can build a single pyramid that emits all available powers at once.

RANGE OF EFFECTS

Beacon pyramid sizes don't just control the number of powers available from any given beacon, but also the range of the beacon's influence. The larger the pyramid, the longer the range of the beacon's stat buffs.

The radius of a beacon is a square that forms around the pyramid. This extends outward for the same length horizontally and vertically downwards. The buff's influence follows the beam of light all the way to the top of the world – that's 256 blocks high if the beacon is at the very bottom of the world.

So, if you build a three-level pyramid, a beacon's influence will extend 40 blocks in each direction, and downwards, and up to 256 blocks upwards along the light.

Items are needed to activate various beacon buffs

WINNING MINECRAFT:
REACHING THE END

Even though Minecraft is an open-world game, those who play long enough will recognise a distinct path to the finale, which involves facing the game's most dangerous (and impressive) foe, then living to tell the tale. If you haven't got time to discover the path yourself, feel free to follow our guide instead. Be warned, though – there are massive spoilers ahead!

THE PATH TO THE END

Defeating the End is only half the struggle. To complete the game, you first have to fulfil the conditions necessary the enter the End. What follows is an (abbreviated) description of what you must do:

Begin a new game in Survival mode. You'll spawn in the Overworld, and must survive long enough to craft tools and armour. Using your skills and weaponry, search the lowest depths of the map to acquire diamonds and with them the means to mine obsidian. Use obsidian to create a portal to the Nether.

When you arrive in the Nether, seek out a Nether fortress containing a blaze spawner. Kill some blazes and collect at least six blaze rods, although more will give you a greater margin for error and the chance to craft other items. Return with them to the Overworld. Turn blaze rods into blaze powder and combine them with an ender pearl to create at least 12 eyes of ender. Use an eye of ender to locate a stronghold by throwing it and watching the direction in which it

A thrown eye of ender showing the way to the nearest stronghold

travels (which will be towards the nearest stronghold)

In the stronghold, use your entire set of eyes of ender to activate an ender portal by placing one in

An active End portal

each of the 12 ender portal blocks. If the portal successfully activates, you now have access to the End, a special realm separate from the Overworld, similar to the Nether but with one major attribute: it's the home of the ender dragon.

WELCOME TO THE END

The End is a small, dark, largely featureless realm with no day/night cycle and very few block types. Most blocks behave identically to the Overworld, with a few notable exceptions: plants won't grow, maps, compasses and clocks won't function properly, beds will explode, and Nether portals won't activate.

Once you enter the End, you'll be standing on top of a 5x5 square platform of obsidian. You may be surrounded by the terrain of the End, but it's also possible to appear on a platform some distance away, which will require you to build your own bridge to a safer vantage point. Anything built directly on top of this platform will be destroyed when a player enters the End, and all End portals in the Overworld lead to the same point in the End.

It's recommended that players bring a plentiful supply of obsidian with them, as this is the only type of block mineable from the Overworld that can't

be destroyed by the ender dragon, making it useful for building structures. A diamond pickaxe is also useful, because it's possible for the player to spawn beneath the End's terrain, surrounded by End stone, which must be mined to reach the surface.

There are only two ways to leave the End. You can die, which will cause you to drop anything you're carrying and return you to your most recent spawn point. Or you can defeat the ender dragon. To aid you in the latter objective, the ender dragon's health is constantly displayed at the top of the screen as long as you remain in the End.

As you arrive in the End, the ender dragon will spawn high in the air, floating above the End's obsidian pillars. Each of these is topped with an ender crystal that can replenish the ender dragon's

The End isn't a nice place to be

The ender dragon being healed by an ender crystal

health. To successfully kill the ender dragon, it's a good tip to first deactivate these crystals. Destroying ender crystals is simple, as they'll explode on contact. A bow and arrow will take care of them.

Defeating the ender dragon is still incredibly difficult and will likely require several players to make the attempt at once. When threatened, the ender dragon will bombard players with powerful, block-destroying attacks, making it difficult to stay alive or build useful structures without support.

If defeated, the ender dragon will dissolve, creating an exit portal composed of indestructible bedrock that returns you to the Overworld. At the same time, a dragon egg will spawn. When the player enters the exit portal, the End poem and credits will roll. Then the player will return to the Overworld. It's possible to return to the End, but the dragon won't spawn again and the exit portal will remain in place.

SLAYING THE DRAGON

Even after destroying the ender crystals, killing the ender dragon is a difficult process. There are many strategies that can be employed to help make this easier. Here are a few:

Method 1: Destroying an ender crystal while the ender dragon is being healed will cause the dragon to take damage. Rather than destroying crystals in advance, wait until the dragon is being affected before shooting it with a projectile weapon.

Method 2: Wait until the ender dragon charges at you, then attack its head using a bow. The dragon's impact will cause damage, so you'll need high armour, ideally with strong enchantments, to survive long enough.

Method 3: Wait until the ender dragon charges at you, then side-step at the last possible moment, attacking its head using a sword or other melee weapon. This technique isn't recommended, because avoiding damage is very, very difficult. Note that sword enchantments don't affect the ender dragon.

You should bring a lot of ammo to the End or, ideally, a bow with an infinity enchantment. All kinds of projectiles damage the dragon, including snowballs and eggs.

Note that unlike endermen, the ender

An ender crystal exploding. That cheap junk breaks the first time you shoot an arrow at it

dragon is immune to fire and water damage, but water can be used to create an area in which endermen can't reach the player.

THE DRAGON EGG

The dragon egg is a unique block that spawns once per game. It teleports when struck, meaning it's difficult to collect. It currently serves no function other than to act as a trophy.

When clicked, a dragon egg will teleport several blocks away. The egg can teleport anywhere within a 15-block radius (on the X and Z axis) or seven blocks on the Y axis. They're affected by gravity and will fall to the ground if unsupported. Dragon eggs won't teleport into solid blocks, but anyone attempting to collect one should be careful to cover up the exit portal – if an egg falls in, it will disappear

The death throes of an ender dragon (spoiler!)

forever! Be careful if the egg spawns next to the edge of the End too – eggs can accidentally teleport into the void.

The only way to pick up a dragon egg is to trick it into falling onto a block that won't support it, such as a torch. The easiest way to do this is to place a torch two blocks beneath it, then destroy the block immediately beneath it. When the egg hits the torch, it will cause pop from a block into a collectable resource. The block can then be placed like any other normal block. A piston placed beneath a dragon egg can also achieve the same effect by pushing it up into the air and letting it fall back down.

CONSOLE NOTES

The console version of the End has a few minor differences in the End. Specifically, the ender dragon, after it takes enough damage, will hover and attack with acid breath. Otherwise, the fight is largely the same.

The newly created exit portal. A dragon egg is visible atop the central pillar

The dragon egg can be pushed by a piston so you can pick it up. If it falls into the portal, it will be on the other side

WINNING MINECRAFT: THE WITHER

If the ender dragon just isn't enough for you, why not challenge the game's second boss, the wither?

Although the ender dragon is the pinnacle of Minecraft most adventurers want to reach and conquer, there's another dangerous foe waiting in the wings to be bested, and this foe has to be created by those who wish to destroy it. Yes, you'll become Minecraft's very own Dr Frankenstein, as you have to build and breathe life into the powerful beast known as the wither.

A dangerous and agile boss mob, the wither is a three-headed monstrosity that resembles a skeleton's torso. It flies around the world shooting wither skulls at anything that moves and can cause a great deal of damage. The wither has 100 more health points than the ender dragon, a total of 300 units, and on Hard it hits even harder than the End's boss. Its wither skull projectiles can also cause the wither status effect, making your life much more difficult.

Luckily, the wither doesn't make use of health regenerating beacons atop obsidian towers, which is a small comfort, as it more than makes up for this with sheer aggression and brute force. If you're going to defeat this beast, you'll need to come prepared. Unlike the ender dragon, the wither can be fought in the Overworld, so if you die it will still be flying around.

PREPARING FOR THE WITHER

Before you actually build the wither, which we'll cover soon, you really should ensure you're ready for the task, as you did with the ender dragon. As the wither does all sorts of damage, and has plenty of life, you're going to need plentiful supplies – this can be a long, drawn-out battle.

Essentials include diamond armour, sword, and a bow and plenty of arrows. These should be enchanted if possible, with the sword having high-level smite, and the bow boasting a power enchantment. Your armour should have Protection IV applied, as this can nullify the wither effect.

Bring plenty of healing potions (Tier II), some golden apples and, if you can, wolves and items to summon golems. These won't really help to damage the wither out in the open, but can distract it, making your job easier.

Finally, whatever you do, don't create the wither anywhere near your home. If you don't beat it on the first try, it will still be around and will lay waste to your home as it attempts to get to you. That includes killing all of your livestock and so on. Always travel far away from any important locations to summon the wither.

BUILDING THE WITHER

Before you can actually build the wither, you'll need the materials it takes to construct it. These include four blocks of soul sand and three wither skulls. These can all be found in the Nether. Soul sand can be dug up, and wither skulls are very rarely dropped by wither skeletons. So, you'll need to do some questing and find these first.

Once you have the items, find a suitable location to summon the wither and place the soul sand in a T shape. Then, place each wither skull on the top. As soon as you lay the last skull (skulls have to be placed last or the wither won't spawn), the wither will appear and glow blue. At this point, it's charging up and invulnerable, so don't attack. Instead, make like Monty Python and run away. When the wither fully charges up, it releases a massive explosion that destroys anything it envelops, including you.

Once it's exploded, the wither will then take to the skies and start to attack... anything! Yes, if it moves, the wither will attack it. This fact can help you, as if you summoned golems or brought some wolves, you may have some allied distractions. You'll need them too, because anything that takes the wither's attention from you is a help.

The most basic tactic to fight the wither is to simply keep moving and shooting it with arrows, healing when needed. When you weaken the wither enough (around 50%), it will enter the 'armour' mode and become immune to potions and arrows. From this point, you'll need to run in with your enchanted sword to do more damage and finish it off. There isn't much more to it really, at least not in a straight out-and-out fight. The more cunning Minecraft players out there, however, use more devious methods.

To build the wither, place soul sand in a T shape and cap it with three wither skulls

When the wither's health drops to half, it enters 'armour' mode and can only be damaged by melee attacks

A very easy and admittedly cheap way to beat the wither is to dig a small room, around 15x15x3. You could build one, but the explosion caused by the wither's spawning destroys most blocks, including obsidian, so a deep, underground room is better. Then, inside this room create a flock of iron golems; 15 or 20 should do it. Once done, summon the wither and go at it. With an army of golems hammering away alongside you (the room is only 3 high so the wither shouldn't be able to escape), the wither should be dead in no time.

Other methods can involve setting up TNT traps and using long, thin tunnels to slowly

The wither's initial explosion puts creepers to shame

whittle a pursuing wither's health down. It should also be noted that the wither is actually harmed by health splash potions and healed by harming potions. So, if you have some spare health splash potions, during the first half of the fight let fly with them – just don't get them confused with potions of harm, or the fight could last a lot longer!

Once you've beaten the wither, grab the Nether star it drops to make beacons.

MINECRAFT:

Right then! Before we get to the very end of this book, we've just got space to explore some of the game's more advanced and top secret features! This is very much for more advanced and confident Minecraft players, but as always it's worth a look anyway. You never know, there might something you want to try already!

For a start, we're going to take a look at some of the secret blocks that you can find in the game, and how you can get your paws on them! Then, we're really lifting up the hood and going into some of the technical tweaks and settings you can apply. On the PC version, there's an awful lot you can do to affect the performance of the game and its visual look. So, we're going to be taking you through all of that.

And then? We're going to talk about playing online! Minecraft Realms is a brilliant way to extend the Minecraft fun, and we're getting to grips with it at the end of this chapter! If you've never played Minecraft on a server with friends before, there's a whole side of the mighty Minecraft that you've simply never seen!

As you might have guessed, that's an awful lot of stuff that we've got to talk about again, so turn the page and we'll get cracking with secret blocks and items!

114-117   SECRET BLOCKS

118-121   TECHNICAL SECRETS

122-125   SETTINGS AND TWEAKS

126-129   PLAYING MINECRAFT ONLINE

ADVANCED SECRETS

SECRET BLOCKS

Exposed diorite and andesite on a hillside

How to craft diorite

Naturally occurring granite in a rockface

Recent updates added new stone blocks that generate where you'd previously have found regular ones. The blocks – diorite, andesite and granite – look simple, but can be crafted into polished blocks that can't be found elsewhere. All three of these blocks have the same strength as normal, but can't be turned into slabs, bricks and walls, and don't have chiselled variants. It's possible these features will be added, though.

DIORITE: Forms naturally underground, or can be crafted from cobblestone with two blocks and two pieces of Nether quartz, which uses up the Nether quartz and gives you two diorite blocks. Turn it into a polished block by crafting four blocks together.

ANDESITE: Also found underground, or you can make two blocks by combining one diorite block with one cobblestone block. You can also turn andesite into polished andesite by crafting four blocks together.

GRANITE: Like the others, granite forms underground or can be made by crafting diorite with a piece of Nether quartz. This uses up the Nether quartz and gives you polished granite.

CRAFTED STRUCTURAL BLOCKS

While you can find simple structural blocks, there are at least two that you can only get by crafting:

STONE WALLS

Stone walls act like fences, but aren't generated as part of villages or mines. You can make six wall blocks or six mossy wall blocks by crafting together six cobblestone or six mossy cobblestone (but not a mixture of both).

& ITEMS

An open gate

Mossy and normal walls connecting

Like fences, players and mobs can't jump over walls, and the way they're crafted means they're more efficient for keeping mobs away than placing two cobblestone blocks on top of one another. Take care, though, skeletons can shoot over walls and fences more easily than two cobblestone blocks. You can place walls on top of one another to create a lattice effect, and if you place two pieces of wall diagonally next to one another they won't join up but players can't walk through them.

FENCE GATES

Crafted from two wooden plank blocks with two sticks on either side, fence gates can be opened and closed, but can't be jumped over. They can be controlled by redstone power, and open both inward and outward, depending on where they're pushed from. If you place a fence gate next to a wall or fence they'll connect up, but they won't connect to glass panes or iron railings. The type of wood planks used determines the colour.

REDSTONE-BASED BLOCKS

Redstone dust is easy to find and use, but there are two types of block that you can only get by crafting it.

REDSTONE LAMPS

You can make a redstone lamp by crafting a glowstone block with four pieces of redstone dust. The lamp looks similar to glowstone, but it can be turned on and off by a redstone charge. When active, it produces a light level of 15 – the most any block can produce in the game, and equal to glowstone and Jack 'o' lanterns.

BLOCK OF REDSTONE

By crafting nine pieces of redstone together, you can make a block. Its primary purpose is for storing and transporting large amounts of redstone dust, because they stack in piles of 64 (like redstone dust), but each block contains nine times as much redstone. To turn a block of redstone back into redstone dust, you need a crafting table – placing the block then mining it will cause you to collect the block again. Redstone blocks also work as an always-on power supply that isn't affected by lava and water.

Prismarine is prized as a decorative block because of its animated texture that cycles through several colours over roughly five minutes. It has the same hardness as stone and other stone-like minerals.

SEA LANTERNS

You can find sea lanterns in ocean monuments, but, again, they're quite hard to collect due to their position. To mine one, you need a silk touch pickaxe. Any other tool will shatter it into prismarine crystals, which you can collect and reuse. Combine five crystals with four prismarine shards to create a sea lantern, which will emit light level 15 even above water. You can also collect prismarine crystals by killing guardians and elder guardians, which will also leave the original lanterns in the monument where they may be useful.

RESOURCE STORAGE

Some resource blocks form naturally in the Overworld. Others, such as lapis lazuli and coal, must be created by crafting. They're useful because they allow you to carry and store larger amounts of an item in a single inventory slot, but there are other interesting types of mineral block.

BLOCK OF QUARTZ

You can make blocks of quartz – in several patterns – out of Nether quartz. While popular for decoration, they can't be crafted back into quartz, so they're no good as storage!

UNDERWATER BLOCKS

There isn't much of interest under the sea, but the latest version of Minecraft has added ocean monuments. This means there are now some unique and rare blocks that can't be found anywhere else, and which can't be crafted.

PRISMARINE

Ocean monuments are made almost entirely out of prismarine and, while it's possible to mine prismarine directly if you have a silk touch pickaxe, its underwater location and large number of nearby enemies make this difficult to do. When you mine prismarine using normal tools, it breaks into prismarine shards, which you can combine back into various types of block:

- Craft four shards together to get one block
- Craft nine shards together to make prismarine bricks
- Craft eight shards with an ink sac to get one block of dark prismarine

Crafting four quartz pieces creates a standard block of quartz, which looks like a light grey block. Craft three quartz blocks together, and you can make six quartz slabs, then craft two of those into a chiselled quartz block, which has a maze-like pattern on the surface. If you craft two blocks of quartz together, you create two blocks of pillar quartz blocks, which have a vertical pattern that makes them look like roman pillars when stacked.

BLOCK OF IRON

Nine pieces of iron can be turned into a block of iron and used in the creation of anvils or as part of the body of iron golems. Like diamond, emerald and gold blocks, they can also power beacons.

SLIME BLOCKS

Slimeballs can be crafted as part of leads, magma cream and sticky pistons. Craft nine together to make a slime block. This slows down mobs and players that walk on them, but if you jump down onto one from a great height you don't take damage; in fact, you'll bounce back up a bit.

DECORATIVE BLOCKS

You can't find most of these blocks in the Overworld, but they're simple to create and fun.

STAINED GLASS & CLAY

Surround any piece of dye (or something that acts as dye, like cocoa beans) with hardened clay or glass blocks to create stained glass or clay, which is useful for decorative items. Stained clay can be found in desert temples and in the rare mesa biome. Stained glass has to be crafted.

BANNERS

Create a basic banner using six wool and one stick. It's then possible to add up to six extra patterns to decorate it. Banners are great for staking your claim to territory in a multiplayer world.

TOP SECRET

Coal blocks make a great fuel for furnaces

Emerald, lapis lazuli and coal storage blocks

A banner in the Overworld

TECHNICAL

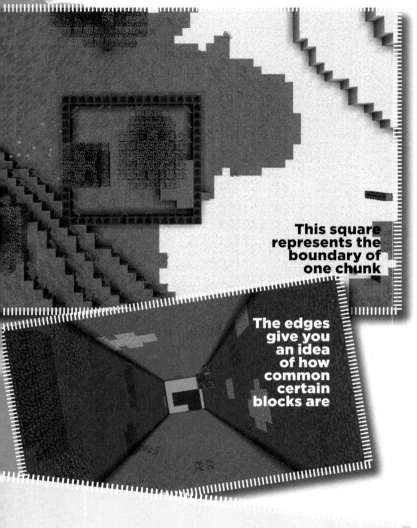

This square represents the boundary of one chunk

The edges give you an idea of how common certain blocks are

Chunks load and unload as you traverse the world

When playing, it helps to have an understanding not just of the game's mechanics, but of the technical underpinnings beneath. A lot of the content that seems random actually has rules governing it, which you can use to your advantage.

CHUNKS

The worlds – the Overworld, the Nether and the End – are divided into chunks. Chunks are 16 blocks square and 256 blocks in height, which in the Overworld means from the bedrock at the bottom to the sky limit at the top. Each chunk contains 65,536 blocks. Chunks are largely a convenient way to store data. Minecraft loads and unloads chunks as you travel so that there's always a manageable amount of world data loaded at any one time. The content of chunks is predetermined by the seed of the world you're playing on and the world algorithm, but chunks don't actually exist until you walk close enough to them for them to be loaded. Once you understand how they work you can use them to inform your game. Any activity on chunks stops as soon as the chunk is unloaded. This is why you can sometimes plant crops, go exploring, then find that they haven't grown as much as you expect when you return to them. So, you can tailor things to remain close to a chunk where crops are growing if you need them quickly.

Certain blocks and mobs are restricted by the chunks that they appear in. The general rule, for instance, is that emerald ore is only generated in the extreme hills biome. However, it is more correct to say that emerald ore only generates in chunks that contain a portion of an extreme hills biome. All this means that it's entirely possible to find emerald ore in any biome adjacent to extreme hills as well.

SECRETS

TOP SECRET

The generation algorithms for all types of ore are restricted to individual chunks, which means there's always a limited amount of each type within every chunk. Diamond ore is only generated once per chunk in veins of 3-8 blocks, so as soon as you find some you can move to another chunk before resuming your search.

You can find out more about what chunk you're in by using the Debug screen (of which more later). Since chunks are the unit of mapping in Minecraft, it's possible to use utilities to transport entire chunks from one map to another, which is useful if you're interested in combining things you've built onto one map or exploring new territory without the hassle of travelling long distances.

DEBUG SCREEN

The Debug screen (which PC players can access by pressing F3) shows a lot of information that can be useful in diagnosing problems with your hardware, but it also contains a lot of information that can help you in your day-to-day gaming as well, even though using it might not be in the strict spirit of the game!

The information on the Debug screen, starting line by line from the top left, is as follows:

• **Minecraft version information**

In this case, version 1.8.7 'vanilla' build, which is to say not a nightly, experimental or otherwise modded version.

• **Statistics**

Most of these are highly technical in nature and not of much practical use to players, but at least you can learn what they mean.

On the first line, you see the FPS data. Low FPS values (60 is about normal) explain jerky or stuttering visuals, while the rest of the data includes an explanation as to why FPS rates might be low. If chunks are being updated, see what the frame limit is (marked with a T) and what other graphics settings you might have enabled.

Most of the stats are preceded by an abbreviated letter. Here's what they mean:

C: Chunks rendered over total number of chunks
D: Client-side render distance in chunks
pC: Pending chunks to be processed
pU: Pending uploads to video card
aB: Available buffers for processing
E: Number of rendered entities over total entities
B: Currently unused. Should always be zero.
I: Number of invisible entities
P: Number of particles on screen
All: Total number of loaded entities, including mobs and dropped items
MultiPlayerChunkCache: The most chunks that will be loaded.

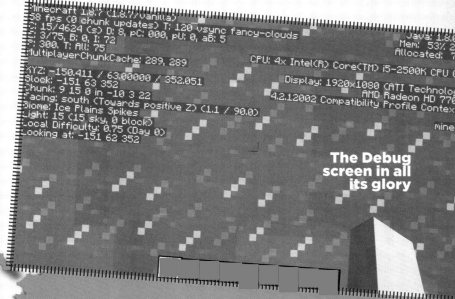

The Debug screen in all its glory

119

Page 2 of 2
Monument -249 63
-2343
Mine -471 39 -1737
Dungeon -564 32
-1848
VilPortal -143 72 951
Portal 3 1440 43 1295
Island Shack 1377 63
1314_

Sign   Done

You could even use a book to note down co-ordinates

You can view the decay status of leaves on the Debug screen

The Debug screen helps you find biome boundaries

- **Location data**

This is the stuff that helps the most, offering several pieces of data about where you are in the world.

You see two versions of the XYZ/Block co-ordinates. The XYZ is your position, whereas the Block co-ordinates are the same values for the block you're standing on. These are useful numbers, because they give your absolute position in the world map. Compasses point back to the world's spawn point, so it's hard to navigate long distances using them, but the co-ordinates are always the same. The X co-ordinate gives you your location east of X=0 (negative numbers are west), the Y co-ordinate gives your altitude in blocks about Y=0 (sea level in The Overworld is Y=63), and the Z co-ordinate gives you your location south of Z=0 (negative numbers are north).

The data marked 'Chunk' tells you where you are in a chunk (the first three numbers) and where that chunk lies within the overall world (the second three numbers). 'Facing' tells you the direction your character is facing, as well as the horizontal and vertical rotation of your head in brackets afterwards.

The Biome gives you the type of biome you're in. Light tells you the light level where your feet are. The number before the word 'sky' tells you how much of this light is from the sky, while the number before the word 'block' tells you how much of the light is from other sources.

Local Difficulty tells you the difficulty setting of your current chunk. It also tells you, in brackets, how many in-game days you've been in the current world. 'Looking at' shows you the XYZ co-ordinates of the block you currently have selected in the crosshair. In the bottom right, it will also show specifics about that block, including its name and other information.

- **Machine data**

The right-hand column is given over to system data, including the Java version the software is running, the amount of memory available and allocated, the model and speed of the PC's CPU, the resolution and GPU, and the profile version. Most of this is useful for tracking and locating performance problems, but not otherwise.

LOCAL DIFFICULTY

As well as its standard difficulty settings, the game has local difficulty effects that are dependent on player and world behaviour.

We've noted elsewhere that the moon's phases can affect mob behaviour. The most prominent of these effects is how slimes spawn in swamp biomes. On a full moon, there's a 100% chance that slimes will spawn. On a gibbous moon, it's 75%, on a half moon it drops to 50%, and on a crescent moon it drops to 25%. New moons give slimes 0% chance of spawning.

The moon's phases also act on local difficulty calculations in the same way. The exact algorithm for local difficulty is a complex one based on several factors, including the phase of the moon, the amount of time the current chunk has been inhabited, the total play time in the world, and the current difficulty setting, but they all combine to give the chunk a single difficulty value within a certain range. Local difficulty ranges from a 0.75 minimum on Easy mode to a 6.75 maximum on Hard. The higher the local difficulty, the more chance of certain effects occurring. Things like mob damage and health are affected by the main difficulty setting only. Local difficulty amplifies the chances of things like mobs spawning with enchanted or stronger equipment, the chance of zombies and skeletons being able to pick up items, and slimes spawning at full size.

The effect of all this is that the first time you enter a chunk it remains relatively safe, but the longer you spend in a single chunk the harder it becomes, especially if the moon is full. On easier modes, this effect is hardly noticeable, but it is on higher modes. It's worth noting that the 'inhabited' time of a chunk is cumulative for players. The maximum value is 50, which can mean 50 hours inhabited by one player, 25 hours by two players, or one hour by 50 players. The maximum playtime value is 21. Essentially, after 21 hours of playing and 50 person hours in a chunk, it can get no more difficult. Move to another chunk and it will suddenly be a lot easier!

The moon's phases have an effect on local difficulty

High local difficulty means mobs can spawn with good equipment

Keep moving, and local difficulty will stay low

SETTINGS &

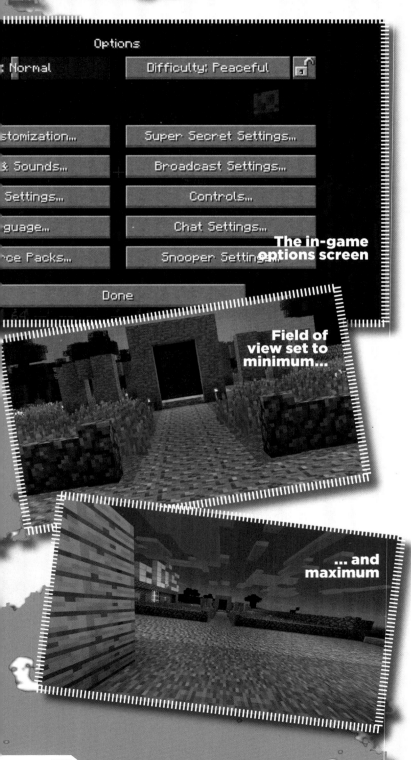

Options

: Normal   Difficulty: Peaceful

stomization...   Super Secret Settings...

& Sounds...   Broadcast Settings...

Settings...   Controls...

guage...   Chat Settings...

ce Packs...   Snooper Settings...

Done

The in-game options screen

Field of view set to minimum...

... and maximum

Minecraft has a big set of options to customise the game. Let's take a look. We've used the PC version as a base, but most appear in other versions too.

OPTIONS SCREEN

This mostly gives you access to other option screens, but does contain the FOV settings. FOV stands for 'Field of View' and determines how far around yourself you can see. Setting it low gives you a very immersive 'first person' feel, while higher settings allow you to see more but cause fisheye distortion at the image's edges.

If a world is loaded, you'll also see the difficulty settings. This mostly controls mob strength and behaviour. On Peaceful difficulty, there are no hostile mobs in the game and the food bar doesn't deplete (you can still die from things like falling and drowning). On Easy difficulty, spiders can't poison you and it's easy to make creepers stop attacks. On Normal, players will be injured until they have just one health point if their food bar isn't refilled. On Hard, it's possible to starve to death, zombies can break through doors, and spiders can spawn with status effects that make them deadlier.

SKIN CUSTOMISATION OPTIONS

Options here allow you to change whether each portion of a custom skin is loaded from your online profile. Note that this may be overridden by mods that change the player skin or model.

MUSIC & SOUNDS OPTIONS

This lets you change the volume of individual parts of the soundscape – ideal if you don't like the sound of zombies, but don't want to play in silence. If you do like silence, you can also modify the master volume.

TWEAKS

VIDEO SETTINGS OPTIONS

This options screen is probably the most complex of them all and also the one with the greatest potential to alter the performance of your game, so it makes sense to learn what its various settings do!

The **Graphics** setting allows you to choose between 'Fast' and 'Fancy'. Fast graphics will give you a higher frame ate, but fancy graphics look better. In Fast mode, clouds are opaque, and some semi-transparent blocks, such as leaf blocks, become solid.

Smooth Lighting changes whether lighting effects are applied as a gradient across a block or whether each block has its own light level. It's sometimes known as 'ambient occlusion'. Switching it off or lowering the setting will improve framerates on slow machines, especially ones without a separate graphics card.

Turning **3D Anaglyph** on and off allows players to use red/blue 3D glasses to achieve a 3D effect.

GUI Scale changes whether the menu and in-game HUD resize based on the game's resolution and screen size, or stay at a fixed size regardless of how they change.

The **Clouds** setting changes whether clouds are rendered volumetric (Fancy), flat (Fast) or not at all (off). Cloud opacity isn't affected by this option. Again, turning the detail down or off can improve framerates.

Fullscreen changes whether the game is windowed or not. You can quickly and easily toggle this option by pressing F11 under the default control scheme.

Mipmap Levels determine how smooth textures look in the distance. High mipmap

levels use more RAM, but low ones can give a worse framerate, so leave the setting how it is unless you experience problems.

The **Use VBOs** option refers to an OpenGL feature called Vertex Buffer Objects. If you have a good graphics card, turning this option on can improve framerates by as much as 10% by shifting workload from your CPU and RAM to your graphics card.

Render Distance determines, using game chunks as a measure, how far you can see. The lower this setting, the faster your framerate will be, though the change in viewing distance will be noticeable. Only high-end cards can support higher distance settings.

Max Framerate sets a limit on the game's speed. Changing it won't make your game faster unless you're already hitting the maximum speed, which, at the default of 120fps, is unlikely.

View Bobbing lets you toggle whether the camera bobs up and down as you walk in first-person mode. With no discernible effect on performance, it's all down to personal preference!

Render distance: low (left) vs high (right)

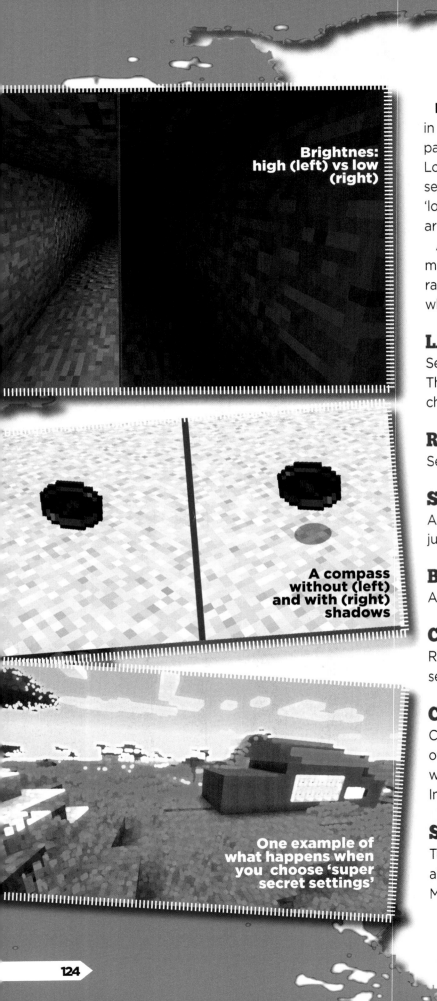

Brightnes: high (left) vs low (right)

A compass without (left) and with (right) shadows

One example of what happens when you choose 'super secret settings'

Brightness can be altered to see more detail even in dark areas. Particle settings determine how many particles you see, including during weather events. Lower settings improve framerates, but on the minimal setting animals won't display hearts when they enter 'love' mode. Turning Vsync on prevents 'tearing' artefacts but lowers the framerate slightly.

Alternate Blocks allows resource packs to include multiple versions of single blocks, which are displayed randomly when rendered. Entity shadows determines whether entities (such as players) cast shadows.

LANGUAGE OPTIONS

Select a different translation of menus and messages. The 'force Unicode font' setting should be switched on if characters or symbols are failing to appear correctly.

RESOURCE PACKS

See available resource packs. Simple.

SUPER SECRET SETTINGS

Apply a random graphical filter to the game. They're just for fun and some dramatically reduce performance.

BROADCAST SETTINGS

Allows you to synchronise your Twitch.tv account.

CONTROLS

Redefine keys for common actions, change mouse sensitivity and activate touchscreen mode.

CHAT SETTINGS

Can be turned on and off, the colours, opacity and size of incoming chat can be changed, and the behaviour with regards to links altered. Activating Reduced Debug Info shows less information on the debug screen.

SNOOPER SETTINGS

Turn on and off the option that sends anonymous data about your PC's hardware and gaming behaviour to Mojang (which is used to help develop the game).

CREATE NEW WORLD OPTIONS

You have lots of options here to determine how your game world looks and behaves when it's generated. Be sure to click 'more world options' to change even more details about it.

The world seed generates a map, and if the seed and game version are the same you can see the same world on different systems. You can leave the seed blank to get a random one. Using a predetermined seed lets you share the basic world with others (useful if you're looking to start near a rare biome or feature).

Generate Structures determines whether you get an all-natural world or one that includes villages, mines, temples, monuments, dungeons and strongholds. Desert wells generate even with structures turned off.

Allow Cheats gives you the option (or not) to use 'cheat' commands. While you can always access the console whether this option is turned on or off, you can't use it for certain things if it's disabled.

Toggling the **Bonus Chest** on or off gives you the option to start with some basic items nearby as soon as you start playing in any game mode.

CONSOLE COMMANDS

The console gives you access to commands that aren't available any other way. To access it, press 't' (to talk) or forward slash '/'. The full list of commands is far too extensive to list here, but here's a list of useful ones for single players. Most only work with cheats enabled!

/gamemode [survival|creative] <player>
Switches between Survival and Creative mode.

/weather [clear|rain|thunder]
Changes weather to the type specified. You can add a duration in seconds to place a limit on the weather.

/time set [day|night]
Automatically changes the time of day to early day or early night. Use a value between 0 and 23999 to get fine control over the position of the sun.

/xp <number>L <player>
Increases the experience of the specified player by the number of levels given.

Villages (and villagers) are generated structures

Not all bonus chests are easy to reach!

PLAYING MINEC

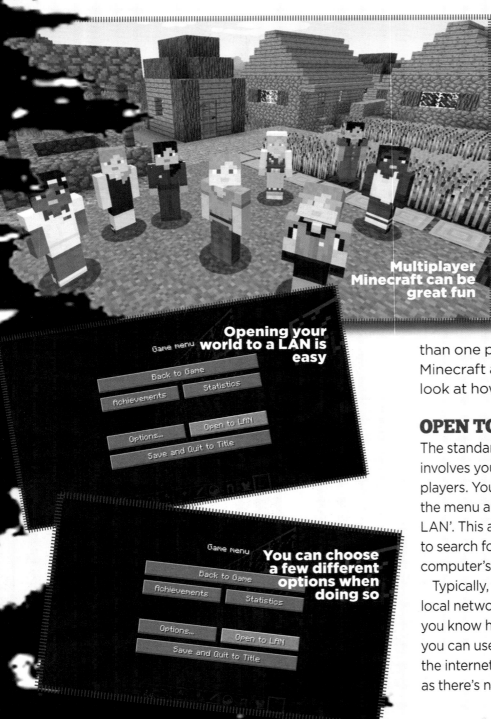

Multiplayer Minecraft can be great fun

Opening your world to a LAN is easy

You can choose a few different options when doing so

Minecraft is great fun solo, but the game really comes into its own when you play it online. The multiplayer capabilities of Minecraft are a big part of its popularity. With multiple players in a single world, you can collaborate with friends on larger structures and resource-collecting expeditions, fight as a team, even deathmatch with one another if you like!

Despite this, the game's online component isn't particularly straightforward or, rather, the number of ways to get online makes it slightly more complex than it has to be. There are several ways you can get more than one person into your world, so (using the PC Minecraft as a guide) we're going to take a brief look at how you might get started with all of them.

OPEN TO LAN

The standard multiplayer experience in Minecraft simply involves you opening your current world up to other players. You can do this by pausing the game to get to the menu and clicking the button that reads 'open to LAN'. This allows any other player on your local network to search for and connect to your server using your computer's local IP address.

Typically, this means machines running on the same local network (i.e. connected to the same router), but if you know how to set up a VPN (virtual private network) you can use the same settings to play with friends over the internet. This is a particularly secure way to play, as there's no chance of anyone stumbling across or

RAFT ONLINE

You have a choice of up to three worlds

REALMS

If you want to share a world with friends that's accessible regardless of whether one person's machine is active and connected or not, a simple way to achieve this is by using Minecraft Realms.

Realms is a subscription-based service run by Mojang that allows players of all abilities to create and administer their own private server. Realms are intended to provide modest online spaces for small groups of friends or family to play together. Each Realm supports up to 20 users and only ten may play at any one time.

Realms is a fairly low-maintenance way to create an online space, as the software is kept up to date for you. It also has the advantage of being official, meaning it's unlikely to disappear unexpectedly. The only requirements are that you have a Mojang account, a paid-for copy of Minecraft and that you are over 13 years of age.

Note that a monthly fee for Minecraft Realms applies, which you'll need to pay.

ACCESSING & CONFIGURING

You can create a realm using the Minecraft Realms sub-menu, accessed from the title screen. It will show a list of any realms you have access to, which includes any you've created and any you've been invited to. If you haven't yet got a realm, click 'buy realm', which will take you through the process of buying one on the official site: minecraft.net/realms.

Once you have one, you have a number of options, drawn from the standard options for Minecraft, though you have the ability to invite existing players to access your world (as long as they have a Mojang account) and you can download your world to access it offline.

Each account comes with three worlds and a slot for a minigame world, offering a selection of prefabricated games. There are also several adventure maps available. Realms are automatically backed up every few days, so if anything goes wrong it's possible to download and restore an earlier version.

It's possible to download Realms for local play

Play Multiplayer

Paul's Minecraft Server
If you get stuff stolen, let me know right away. I'll check the logs & ban someone. PA

Hypixel   22621/26025
Hypixel Network | Build Battle Update!
NEW GAME! → HYPIXEL SKYWARS

MC Legends   919/2500
× MC-Legends Network — PLAYMC.MX ×
-=×=- NEW Prison Gangs! -=×=-

Scanning for games on your local network
o o O

| Join Server | Direct Connect | Add server |
| Edit | Delete | Refresh | Cancel |

Third-party servers let you play with larger groups

The hub areas can be incredibly elaborate

Floating text can give you a pointer on where to go

THIRD-PARTY SERVERS

If you're after an online experience with a bit more personality, try a third-party server. Set up by independent operators, these typically run on their own hosted server and require a bit more technical know-how to set up, although they're still easy enough to access.

While these servers can run the standard Minecraft, they sometimes host additional resource packs or run modded versions. The advantage of joining a third-party server is they host all the necessary modifications for you.

Third-party servers are often unregulated, which means it's easy to meet content that isn't family friendly or fairly administered. Like all online games, identities should be protected during play, and inappropriate activity should be reported to the server's admins. Certainly, any parents allowing their children to use them should supervise them too.

As with many online communities, there are a number of different terms you might encounter, which have specific meanings. 'Anarchy' servers are rule-less free-for-alls with virtually no rules, bar anything that's outright illegal. 'Griefing' is usually explicitly banned or allowed on most large servers and refers to specifically targeting a player for attacks or destroying their work. 'Whitelist' servers are the most regulated: you sign up for an account to use them and rules are enforced.

It's worth paying attention to other statistics, such as a server's uptime (how often is it available?) and its population (do you want to play with thousands of people or just a few?). Most servers are free to connect to, but if you become a regular you may want to donate towards running costs. Most public servers have a reputation system that allows you to receive perks for donating. That might be a special donators-only cape or special tools. If you're looking to get started, there are sites that list popular servers, such as minecraft-server-list.com, minecraftservers.org and minecraft-mp.eu. You do need to be over 13 years of age.

JOINING THIRD-PARTY SERVERS

Joining a third-party server is normally simple. At best, all you have to do is click on the multiplayer button on your home screen then add the server using the IP address or hostname. There are complications that may arise, however. The most common is a difference in the version of Minecraft you have versus the one the server is running. If the two are incompatible, you'll have to download and install the relevant version. Most servers take a while to update to the latest version, so you're most likely to have this problem if a new release has just come out.

The quickest way to fix it is to use the Profile Editor on the Minecraft launcher and change to a compatible version in the Version Selection menu (click on 'Use Latest Version'). Be aware that this will change your main version of Minecraft, though, which may result in you losing compatibility with other servers and your existing saved worlds. If you're changing the version for any long-term purpose, you should instead create a new profile solely for that multiplayer server, so that you can switch to it when you want to play online and maintain your main profile using the latest version.

Once you have the correct profile and have added the server to your list of available games, you should then be able to join without any problems.

Upon joining the server, you'll usually need to have a look around to read the rules and learn the basic commands for that server. Typically, you'll be given a default inventory that allows you to access a wider menu system, and you'll either find instructions written in a book in your inventory or posted on signs around the starting area. If you're confused, don't worry – third-party multiplayer servers are a very different experience to standard Minecraft so some period of adjustment will be necessary. It won't be long before you're as comfortable with them as you are with the basic game – and a whole new catalogue of Minecraft experiences will be open to you!

The GUI on third-party games is often a lot more complex

Signs usually offer instructions to new players

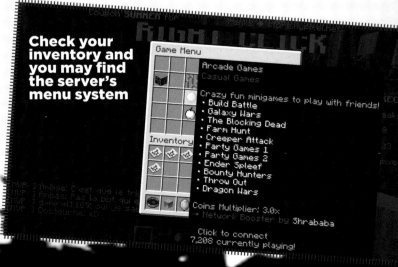

Check your inventory and you may find the server's menu system

MINECRAFT:

Phew! You've found your way to the back of the book, and hopefully that means that you've lost more than a few hours to the majesty of Minecraft on your way here!

However, this part of the guide has been designed so that you can dip in and dip out of it, so it's entirely feasible that you're still in the early stages of the game. Whatever stage you're at, you'll find plenty of useful things here.

Examples? Well, in this appendix section, we've put together some handy reference material for you. We've got our list of block IDs, as well as a comprehensive crafting glossary for you to work your way through!

Also in this appendix, we've got a special look at what's available for those who run the game on a PC. The PC modding community has created all sorts of freely downloadable add-ons for Minecraft and, without a doubt, they're definitely worth exploring. There are assorted skins and updates too, so we've rounded up some of those to give you a flavour of just what's available.

And then that's that! We reach the end of our Minecraft journey – for now! – and wish you many happy hours with the game. Beware the creepersssssss...

132-135   **MODS, SKINS AND UPDATES**

136-139   **BLOCK ID LIST**

140-147   **CRAFTING GLOSSARY**

APPENDIX

MODDING, SKINNING AND UPDATING

Minecraft is an always changing game, and skilled players can make their own mark on the world too

Like a lot of PC games, Minecraft embraces the modding community, and gives people the chance to customise the game to their own liking. These 'mods', or modifications can be applied to the vanilla version of Minecraft, producing all sorts of effects.

You can apply new skins to your avatar, or texture packs (now resource packs) that change the way the entire Minecraft world looks. There are even modifications available that add totally new functionality to the game, actually changing the way it plays.

Authoring these mods requires specialised knowledge and artistic ability, but the game is open to anyone who has the skills. The results of these modifications, however, are open to all, and it's easy enough to apply any modifications to your Minecraft installation, changing your game experience.

SKINS

The most basic form of Minecraft modding is skinning, where you alter the appearance of the main avatar from the usual 'Steve' skin to something else. This can be done by anyone who's purchased the game, and requires no programming knowledge at all. All you need is the character template, which can be downloaded from your Minecraft profile page, and a basic image editor. MS Paint will do the job.

Simply open the base skin then edit it as you wish. Once you've made your changes, save it as

The default reference skin can be edited in any image editor and uploaded into Minecraft

a .png and return to your profile page and upload. After a few seconds, your player skin will be updated to your newly edited version. If you want to return to the standard Steve skin for any reason, simply upload an unedited copy of the reference skin. Easy.

Console owners aren't left out of this either; you can obtain skin packs that can be added to your copy. Then, in-game, go to the options screen and you'll be able to change your skin for one of the ones in the pack (the game comes with a basic pack built in). Sadly, these packs aren't usually free, but they're cheap and feature skins based on other licences, like Halo, Mass Effect, and The Avengers.

RESOURCE PACKS

Replacing the older, now defunct texture packs as of the 1.6 update, resource packs are a means to modify aesthetic elements. This is most commonly demonstrated by packs that change the look of the whole game, adding different visual styles along with higher-resolution textures.

These packs can change textures on blocks, weapons, menus screens and even the main title screen. They alter enemy appearances and generally turn the Minecraft world into a whole new place. There are packs that give the world a photo-realistic look, with detailed grass and stone textures, and there are more outlandish packs that can give Minecraft a steam punk makeover, or make everything look distinctly medieval. There are many to choose from, you just have to have a mooch around the internet to find them.

Unlike texture packs, resource packs also have the option of including new sound, music and language files. This gives modders even more scope to change the whole Minecraft experience, adding new sound effects, and even narration and game event-specific audio when paired up with the 'playsound' command. This, when paired with a command block, can be used to trigger custom audio in-game.

What's more, Mojang has made it easy for end users to use these modifications. To equip your copy of the game with a new resource pack, just download one from the many websites that host such packs (making sure it's compatible with the current version of Minecraft), then extract it into its own folder within the '.minecraft\resourcepacks' folder.

Then, when in the game, simply go to Options\Resource Packs and click the new resource pack you wish to use. After a few seconds, the pack will load and your copy of Minecraft will change, depending on the resource pack. To return to vanilla Minecraft at any time, select the default option from the same menu.

You should note, however, that all pre-1.6 texture packs no longer work with Minecraft, due to the switch to

Mobs are also changed by various resource packs

The exact same house exterior, with three different resource packs applied

And the same house interior using three different packs

resource packs. If you still have any of these and want to continue to use them, you'll need to grab the Texture Ender from Mojang (s3.amazonaws.com/Minecraft. Download/utilities/TextureEnder. jar). This will convert older texture packs, such as the impressive Von Doom pack, into usable resource packs. To use it, simply download it and double-click the jar file. Then, select the folder containing the older texture pack format and let it run. It will create a new resource pack version that'll work perfectly.

If you have older pre-1.5 'stitched' texture packs, grab the Unstitcher from assets.minecraft.net/ unstitcher/unstitcher.jar to convert them. Whereas HD textures previously needed modding tools like MCPatcher, Minecraft 1.5 introduced support for HD.

MODS

Full modifications do more than simply alter the visual appearance of Minecraft; their effects can totally change the game. These mods can range from simple game tweaks and performance enhancements to new gameplay mechanics, including entirely new worlds to explore.

Because of the often extensive changes made to the core game, mods are always used at a person's own risk. As the changes made are large and can actually make Minecraft unstable, Mojang doesn't officially support them, so any issues that arise with your game after using a mod won't be looked into by the official developers. However, Mojang is working on the Plugin API, called Workbench, which will make it

Some packs go for realism instead of fantasy

easier for mods to be developed and installed, without having to mess around with the Minecraft central .jar file. Although still in development at the time of writing, a version of it can be found on Mojang's website at https://github.

Mods like Aether drastically change the game, adding new dimensions

com/Mojang/Minecraft-API.

Until this API is released, users have to enlist the services of unsupported, third-party tools such as ModLoader and Forge to install modifications. For this reason, it's highly advised that you

Like artwork? You'll find all sorts in resource packs

Even inventory and crafting screens can be altered

make a backup of your Minecraft installation before attempting any modding. To do this, simply make a copy of the minecraft.jar file. This can be replaced should anything go wrong, which is very possible even with the smallest of modifications. To back up everything, including your worlds, copy the whole .minecraft folder.

Also, even if you mod the game successfully and everything works, when the core game is updated by Mojang there's a very good chance it will break the mod, which may cause more troubles. At the very least, a new version of the mod will need to be installed.

If you do intend to use mods, always make sure you're careful. It has been known for some mods to contain malicious content, designed to perform nefarious acts, such as stealing usernames and passwords. It's best to always stick to popular mods, and research a new mod using the official forums and other review sites before you load one up.

There are tons of mods available, some much more popular than others, and as already mentioned some of these can add useful features to make the game easier to play, such as the Not Enough Items mod, which shows you recipes for everything you can

create, amongst other things. Other mods add new worlds, like Aether, which adds a new sky dimension for you to explore, complete with new blocks, items and mobs. It even features dungeons with bosses. Other mods are even more ambitious. The Mists of RioV, for example, adds a massive amount of new items, mobs and game mechanics, including two alternate worlds.

Some mods, like OptiFine, add greater render distances, lighting effects and even make Minecraft run more smoothly, which can be useful for those with slower machines.

UPDATES

Minecraft, even without the use of mods or resource packs, is always changing, and Mojang is always releasing new updates to enhance the Minecraft experience. Some updates are simply small bug fixes or tweaks, whilst others are huge overhauls that add a slew of new functionality. Major updates such as the 1.5 'Redstone' update and the 1.6.1 'Horse' update greatly changed the game, adding new items and gameplay elements. At the time this guide was written, Minecraft's version was 1.8.6.

Due to the regularity of these updates, as mentioned in the Mods section above, it's often tricky to play around with Minecraft using mods and the like. Future updates can break the game if it's modified outside of Mojang's offices.

Console versions also feature updates from developer 4J Studios. These come in the form of Title Updates, and are by 2015 were up to TU24 on Xbox 360, CU13 on Xbox One, 1.16 on PS3, and 1.16 on PS4.

There are always rumours and leaks about various planned and upcoming features being circulated too. For example, future updates could include red dragon mobs, enhanced fishing mechanics, more biomes, more detail in the ocean biome, and even seasons. Now that Microsoft owns the title, who knows how Minecraft will develop in the future?

MINECRAFT
BLOCK IDs

Minecraft is all about blocks, and these blocks have IDs, which are useful to know, so here's a list!

ID: 0 AIR	**1** STONE	**2** GRASS	**3** DIRT	**4** COBBLE-STONE	**5** OAK WOOD PLANK
5.1 SPRUCE WOOD PLANK	**5.2** BIRCH WOOD PLANK	**5.3** JUNGLE WOOD PLANK	**6** OAK SAPLING	**6.1** SPRUCE SAPLING	**6.2** BIRCH SAPLING
6.3 JUNGLE SAPLING	**7** BEDROCK	**8** WATER	**9** STATIONARY WATER	**10** LAVA	**11** STATIONARY LAVA
12 SAND	**13** GRAVEL	**14** GOLD ORE	**15** IRON ORE	**16** COAL ORE	**17** OAK WOOD	**17.1** SPRUCE WOOD	**17.2** BIRCH WOOD	**17.3** JUNGLE WOOD	**18** OAK LEAVES
18.1 SPRUCE LEAVES	**18.2** BIRCH LEAVES	**18.3** JUNGLE LEAVES	**19** SPONGE	**20** GLASS	**21** LAPIS LAZULI ORE	**22** LAPIS LAZULI BLOCK	**23** DISPENSER	**24** SANDSTONE	**24.1** CHISELED SANDSTONE
24.2 SMOOTH SANDSTONE	**25** NOTE BLOCK	**26** BED	**27** POWERED RAIL	**28** DETECTOR RAIL	**29** STICKY PISTON	**30** WEB	**31** TALL DEAD SHRUB	**31.1** TALL GRASS	**31.2** FERN
32 DEAD SHRUB	**33** PISTON	**34** PISTON HEAD	**35** WHITE WOOL	**35.1** ORANGE WOOL	**35.2** MAGENTA WOOL	**35.3** LIGHT BLUE WOOL	**35.4** YELLOW WOOL	**35.5** LIME WOOL	**35.6** PINK WOOL
35.7 GRAY WOOL	**35.8** LIGHT GRAY WOOL	**35.9** CYAN WOOL	**35.10** PURPLE WOOL	**35.11** BLUE WOOL	**35.12** BROWN WOOL	**35.13** GREEN WOOL	**35.14** RED WOOL	**35.15** BLACK WOOL	**37** DANDELION
38 ROSE	**39** BROWN MUSHROOM	**40** RED MUSHROOM	**41** GOLD BLOCK	**42** IRON BLOCK	**43** DOUBLE STONE SLAB	**43.1** DOUBLE SANDSTONE SLAB	**43.2** DOUBLE WOODEN SLAB	**43.3** DOUBLE COBBLESTONE SLAB	**43.4** DOUBLE BRICK SLAB
43.5 DOUBLE STONE BRICK SLAB	**43.6** DOUBLE NETHER BRICK SLAB	**43.7** DOUBLE QUARTZ SLAB	**44** STONE SLAB	**44.1** SANDSTONE SLAB	**44.2** WOODEN SLAB	**44.3** COBBLESTONE SLAB	**44.4** BRICK SLAB	**44.5** STONE BRICK SLAB	**44.6** NETHER BRICK SLAB
44.7 QUARTZ SLAB	**45** BRICK	**46** TNT	**47** BOOKSHELF	**48** MOSSY STONE	**49** OBSIDIAN	**50** TORCH	**51** FIRE	**52** MONSTER SPAWNER	**53** WOOD STAIRS

162 ACACIA WOOD	**5.4** ACACIA PLANKS	**44.8** ACACIA SLAB	**163** ACACIA STAIRS	**162.1** DARK OAK WOOD	**5.5** DARK OAK PLANKS	**44.9** DARK OAK SLAB	**164** DARK OAK STAIRS	**6.4** ACACIA SAPLING	**6.5** DARK OAK SAPLING
54 CHEST	**55** REDSTONE WIRE	**56** DIAMOND ORE	**57** DIAMOND BLOCK	**58** CRAFTING TABLE	**59** WHEAT CROPS	**60** FARMLAND	**61** FURNACE	**62** BURNING FURNACE	**63** SIGN POST
64 WOODEN DOOR BLOCK	**65** LADDER	**66** RAILS	**67** COBBLESTONE STAIRS	**68** WALL SIGN	**69** LEVER	**70** STONE PRESSURE PLATE	**71** IRON DOOR BLOCK	**72** WOODEN PRESSURE PLATE	**73** REDSTONE ORE
74 GLOWING REDSTONE ORE	**75** REDSTONE TORCH (OFF)	**76** REDSTONE TORCH (ON)	**77** STONE BUTTON	**78** SNOW	**79** ICE	**80** SNOW BLOCK	**81** CACTUS	**82** CLAY	**83** SUGAR CANE
84 JUKEBOX	**85** FENCE	**86** PUMPKIN	**87** NETHERRACK	**88** SOUL SAND	**89** GLOWSTONE	**90** PORTAL	**91** JACK 'O' LANTERN	**92** CAKE BLOCK	**93** REDSTONE REPEATER BLOCK (OFF)
94 REDSTONE REPEATER BLOCK (ON)	**95** LOCKED CHEST	**96** TRAPDOOR	**97** STONE (SILVERFISH)	**97.1** COBBLESTONE (SILVERFISH)	**97.2** STONE BRICK (SILVERFISH)	**98** STONE BRICK	**98.1** MOSSY STONE BRICK	**98.2** CRACKED STONE BRICK	**98.3** CHISELED STONE BRICK
99 RED MUSHROOM CAP	**100** BROWN MUSHROOM CAP	**101** IRON BARS	**102** GLASS PANE	**103** MELON BLOCK	**104** PUMPKIN VINE	**105** MELON VINE	**106** VINES	**107** FENCE GATE	**108** BRICK STAIRS
109 STONE BRICK STAIRS	**110** MYCELIUM	**111** LILY PAD	**112** NETHER BRICK	**113** NETHER BRICK FENCE	**114** NETHER BRICK STAIRS	**115** NETHER WART	**116** ENCHANTMENT TABLE	**117** BREWING STAND	**118** CAULDRON
119 END PORTAL	**120** END PORTAL FRAME	**121** END STONE	**122** DRAGON EGG	**123** REDSTONE LAMP (INACTIVE)	**124** REDSTONE LAMP (ACTIVE)	**125** DOUBLE OAK WOOD SLAB	**125.1** DOUBLE SPRUCE WOOD SLAB	**125.2** DOUBLE BIRCH WOOD SLAB	**125.3** DOUBLE JUNGLE WOOD SLAB
126 OAK WOOD SLAB	**126.1** SPRUCE WOOD SLAB	**126.2** BIRCH WOOD SLAB	**126.3** JUNGLE WOOD SLAB	**127** COCOA PLANT	**128** SANDSTONE STAIRS	**129** EMERALD ORE	**130** ENDER CHEST	**131** TRIPWIRE HOOK	**132** TRIPWIRE
133 EMERALD BLOCK	**134** SPRUCE WOOD STAIRS	**135** BIRCH WOOD STAIRS	**136** JUNGLE WOOD STAIRS	**137** COMMAND BLOCK	**138** BEACON BLOCK	**139** COBBLESTONE WALL	**139.1** MOSSY COBBLESTONE WALL	**140** FLOWER POT	**141** CARROTS
142 POTATOES	**143** WOODEN BUTTON	**144** MOB HEAD	**145** ANVIL	**146** TRAPPED CHEST	**147** WEIGHTED PRESSURE PLATE (LIGHT)	**148** WEIGHTED PRESSURE PLATE (HEAVY)	**149** REDSTONE COMPARATOR (INACTIVE)	**150** REDSTONE COMPARATOR (ACTIVE)	**151** DAYLIGHT SENSOR

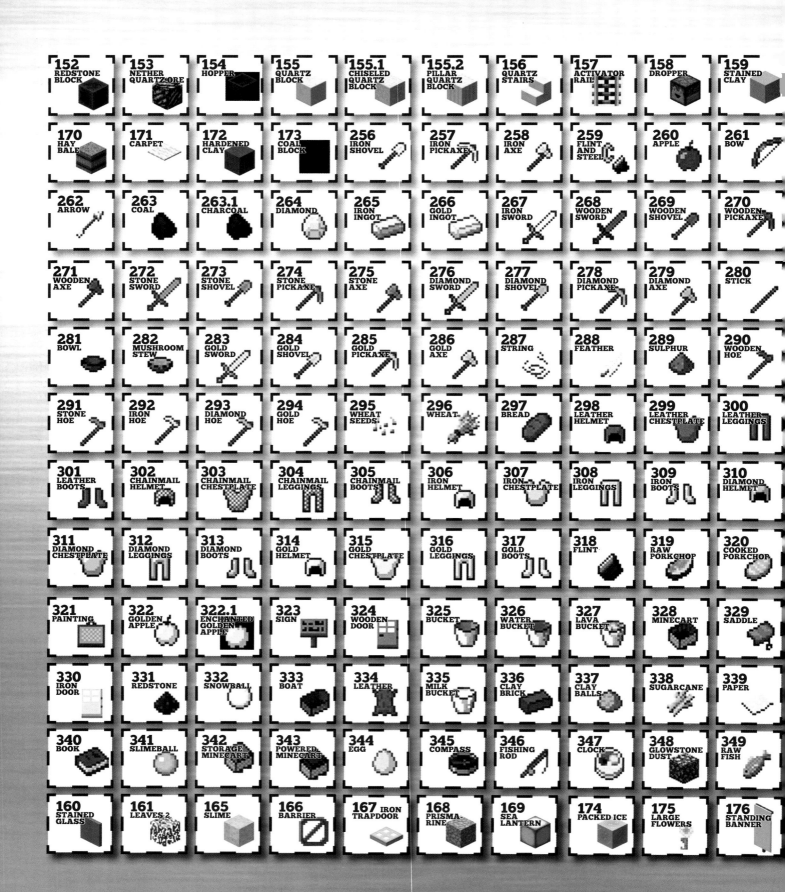

152 REDSTONE BLOCK

153 NETHER QUARTZ ORE

154 HOPPER

155 QUARTZ BLOCK

155.1 CHISELED QUARTZ BLOCK

155.2 PILLAR QUARTZ BLOCK

156 QUARTZ STAIRS

157 ACTIVATOR RAIL

158 DROPPER

159 STAINED CLAY

170 HAY BALE

171 CARPET

172 HARDENED CLAY

173 COAL BLOCK

256 IRON SHOVEL

257 IRON PICKAXE

258 IRON AXE

259 FLINT AND STEEL

260 APPLE

261 BOW

262 ARROW

263 COAL

263.1 CHARCOAL

264 DIAMOND

265 IRON INGOT

266 GOLD INGOT

267 IRON SWORD

268 WOODEN SWORD

269 WOODEN SHOVEL

270 WOODEN PICKAXE

271 WOODEN AXE

272 STONE SWORD

273 STONE SHOVEL

274 STONE PICKAXE

275 STONE AXE

276 DIAMOND SWORD

277 DIAMOND SHOVEL

278 DIAMOND PICKAXE

279 DIAMOND AXE

280 STICK

281 BOWL

282 MUSHROOM STEW

283 GOLD SWORD

284 GOLD SHOVEL

285 GOLD PICKAXE

286 GOLD AXE

287 STRING

288 FEATHER

289 SULPHUR

290 WOODEN HOE

291 STONE HOE

292 IRON HOE

293 DIAMOND HOE

294 GOLD HOE

295 WHEAT SEEDS

296 WHEAT

297 BREAD

298 LEATHER HELMET

299 LEATHER CHESTPLATE

300 LEATHER LEGGINGS

301 LEATHER BOOTS

302 CHAINMAIL HELMET

303 CHAINMAIL CHESTPLATE

304 CHAINMAIL LEGGINGS

305 CHAINMAIL BOOTS

306 IRON HELMET

307 IRON CHESTPLATE

308 IRON LEGGINGS

309 IRON BOOTS

310 DIAMOND HELMET

311 DIAMOND CHESTPLATE

312 DIAMOND LEGGINGS

313 DIAMOND BOOTS

314 GOLD HELMET

315 GOLD CHESTPLATE

316 GOLD LEGGINGS

317 GOLD BOOTS

318 FLINT

319 RAW PORKCHOP

320 COOKED PORKCHOP

321 PAINTING

322 GOLDEN APPLE

322.1 ENCHANTED GOLDEN APPLE

323 SIGN

324 WOODEN DOOR

325 BUCKET

326 WATER BUCKET

327 LAVA BUCKET

328 MINECART

329 SADDLE

330 IRON DOOR

331 REDSTONE

332 SNOWBALL

333 BOAT

334 LEATHER

335 MILK BUCKET

336 CLAY BRICK

337 CLAY BALLS

338 SUGARCANE

339 PAPER

340 BOOK

341 SLIMEBALL

342 STORAGE MINECART

343 POWERED MINECART

344 EGG

345 COMPASS

346 FISHING ROD

347 CLOCK

348 GLOWSTONE DUST

349 RAW FISH

160 STAINED GLASS

161 LEAVES 2

165 SLIME

166 BARRIER

167 IRON TRAPDOOR

168 PRISMA-RINE

169 SEA LANTERN

174 PACKED ICE

175 LARGE FLOWERS

176 STANDING BANNER

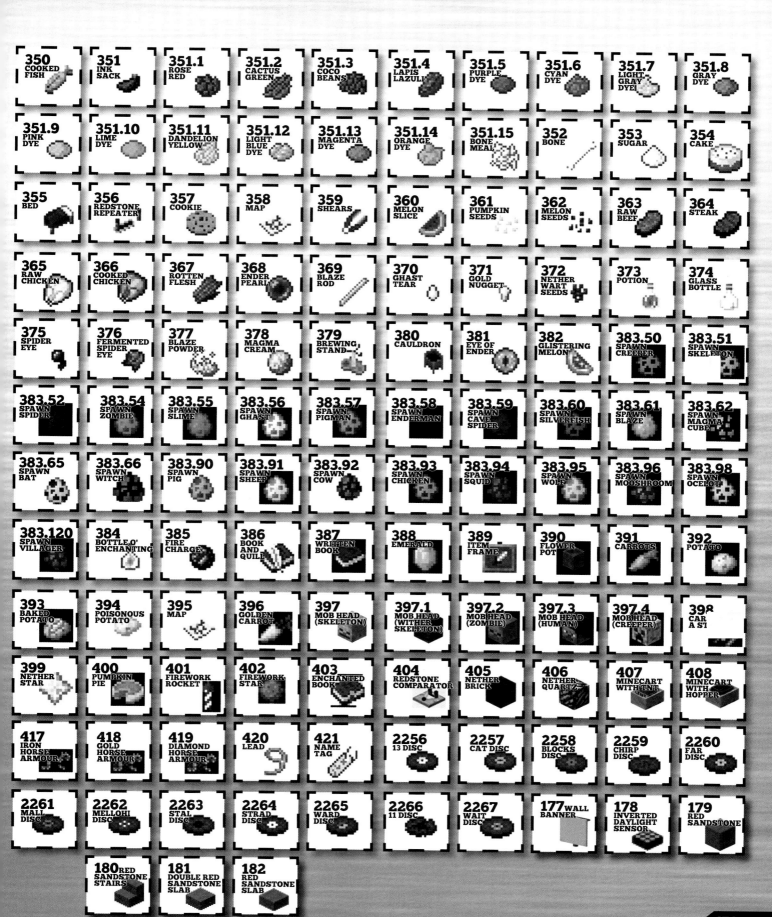

350 COOKED FISH	**351** INK SACK	**351.1** ROSE RED	**351.2** CACTUS GREEN	**351.3** COCO BEANS	**351.4** LAPIS LAZULI	**351.5** PURPLE DYE	**351.6** CYAN DYE	**351.7** LIGHT GRAY DYE	**351.8** GRAY DYE
351.9 PINK DYE	**351.10** LIME DYE	**351.11** DANDELION YELLOW	**351.12** LIGHT BLUE DYE	**351.13** MAGENTA DYE	**351.14** ORANGE DYE	**351.15** BONE MEAL	**352** BONE	**353** SUGAR	**354** CAKE
355 BED	**356** REDSTONE REPEATER	**357** COOKIE	**358** MAP	**359** SHEARS	**360** MELON SLICE	**361** PUMPKIN SEEDS	**362** MELON SEEDS	**363** RAW BEEF	**364** STEAK
365 RAW CHICKEN	**366** COOKED CHICKEN	**367** ROTTEN FLESH	**368** ENDER PEARL	**369** BLAZE ROD	**370** GHAST TEAR	**371** GOLD NUGGET	**372** NETHER WART SEEDS	**373** POTION	**374** GLASS BOTTLE
375 SPIDER EYE	**376** FERMENTED SPIDER EYE	**377** BLAZE POWDER	**378** MAGMA CREAM	**379** BREWING STAND	**380** CAULDRON	**381** EYE OF ENDER	**382** GLISTERING MELON	**383.50** SPAWN CREEPER	**383.51** SPAWN SKELETON
383.52 SPAWN SPIDER	**383.54** SPAWN ZOMBIE	**383.55** SPAWN SLIME	**383.56** SPAWN GHAST	**383.57** SPAWN PIGMAN	**383.58** SPAWN ENDERMAN	**383.59** SPAWN CAVE SPIDER	**383.60** SPAWN SILVERFISH	**383.61** SPAWN BLAZE	**383.62** SPAWN MAGMA CUBE
383.65 SPAWN BAT	**383.66** SPAWN WITCH	**383.90** SPAWN PIG	**383.91** SPAWN SHEEP	**383.92** SPAWN COW	**383.93** SPAWN CHICKEN	**383.94** SPAWN SQUID	**383.95** SPAWN WOLF	**383.96** SPAWN MOOSHROOM	**383.98** SPAWN OCELOT
383.120 SPAWN VILLAGER	**384** BOTTLE O' ENCHANTING	**385** FIRE CHARGE	**386** BOOK AND QUILL	**387** WRITTEN BOOK	**388** EMERALD	**389** ITEM FRAME	**390** FLOWER POT	**391** CARROTS	**392** POTATO
393 BAKED POTATO	**394** POISONOUS POTATO	**395** MAP	**396** GOLDEN CARROT	**397** MOB HEAD (SKELETON)	**397.1** MOB HEAD (WITHER SKELETON)	**397.2** MOB HEAD (ZOMBIE)	**397.3** MOB HEAD (HUMAN)	**397.4** MOB HEAD (CREEPER)	**398** CAR A S1
399 NETHER STAR	**400** PUMPKIN PIE	**401** FIREWORK ROCKET	**402** FIREWORK STAR	**403** ENCHANTED BOOK	**404** REDSTONE COMPARATOR	**405** NETHER BRICK	**406** NETHER QUARTZ	**407** MINECART WITH TNT	**408** MINECART WITH HOPPER
417 IRON HORSE ARMOUR	**418** GOLD HORSE ARMOUR	**419** DIAMOND HORSE ARMOUR	**420** LEAD	**421** NAME TAG	**2256** 13 DISC	**2257** CAT DISC	**2258** BLOCKS DISC	**2259** CHIRP DISC	**2260** FAR DISC
2261 MALL DISC	**2262** MELLOHI DISC	**2263** STAL DISC	**2264** STRAD DISC	**2265** WARD DISC	**2266** 11 DISC	**2267** WAIT DISC	**177** WALL BANNER	**178** INVERTED DAYLIGHT SENSOR	**179** RED SANDSTONE
	180 RED SANDSTONE STAIRS	**181** DOUBLE RED SANDSTONE SLAB	**182** RED SANDSTONE SLAB						

CRAFTING GLOSSARY

Need to know how to make your tools? Can't remember that elusive recipe, or the ingredients you need? Fear not, as all the answers are here

PLEASE NOTE: If you're hungry, and looking for food recipes, check the **Minecraft Cookbook** section of this guide.

BASIC ITEMS

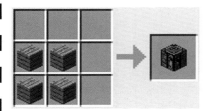

^ **Crafting table**

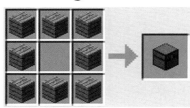

^ **Chest**

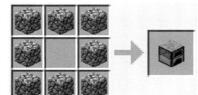

^ **Furnace**

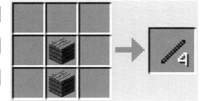

^ **Sticks**

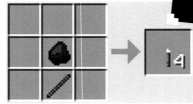

^ **Torches**

^ **Wood planks**
Any wood block

RESOURCE BLOCKS

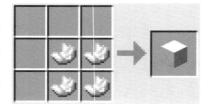

^ **Block of quartz**

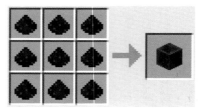

^ **Block of redstone**

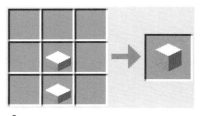

^ **Chiseled quartz block**

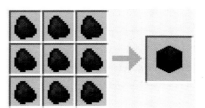

^ **Coal block**

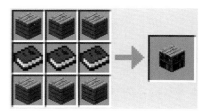

^ **Bookshelf**

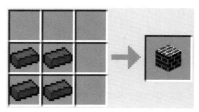

^**Brick block**

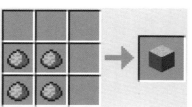

^ **Clay block**

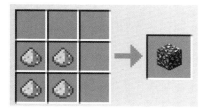

^ Glowstone

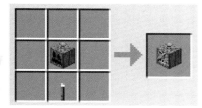

^ Jack 'o' lantern

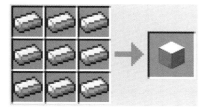

**Ore blocks
Iron, gold, diamond,
lapis lazuli, emeralds,
redstone, coal**

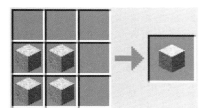

^ Sandstone

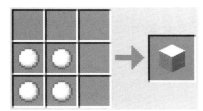

^ Snow block

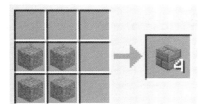

^ Stone brick

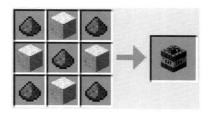

^ TNT block

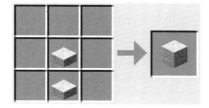

^ Decorative sandstone

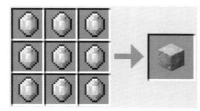

^ Emerald block

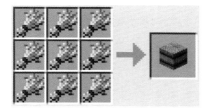

^ Hay bale

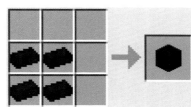

^ Nether brick

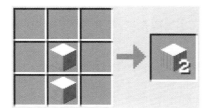

^ Pillar quartz block

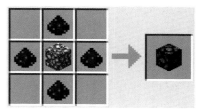

^ Redstone lamp

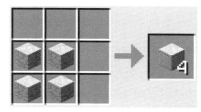

^ Smooth sandstone

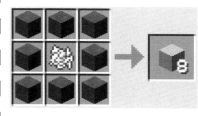

**^ Stained clay
Any dye in the centre**

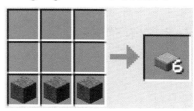

**^ Stone slabs
Cobblestone, brick,
stone, stone brick or
sandstone**

**^ Stone stairs
Cobblestone, brick,
nether brick, stone brick
quartz**

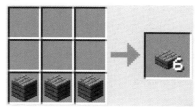

**^ Wood slabs
Any wooden planks**

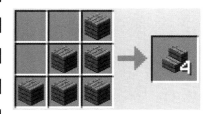

^ Wood stairs

TOOLS

^ Axe
Wooden planks, cobblestone, iron ingots, gold ingots and diamond

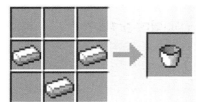

^ Bucket

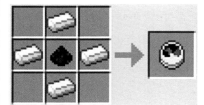

^ Watch

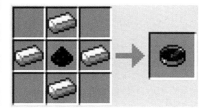

^ Compass

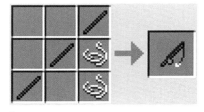

^ Fishing rod

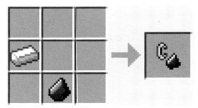

^ Flint and steel

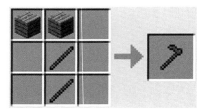

^ Hoe
Wooden planks, cobblestone, iron ingots, gold ingots and diamond

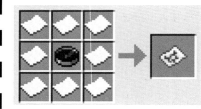

^ Map

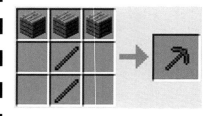

^ Pickaxe
Wooden planks, cobblestone, iron ingots, gold ingots and diamond

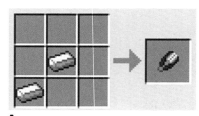

^ Shears

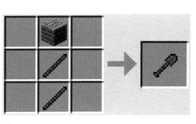

^ Shovel
Wooden planks, cobblestone, iron ingots, gold ingots and diamond

WEAPONS

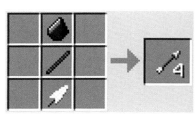

^ Arrows

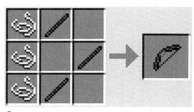

^ Bow

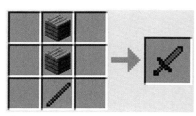

^ Sword
Wooden planks, cobblestone, iron ingots, gold ingots and diamond

ARMOUR

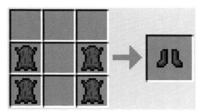

^ Boots
Leather, iron ingots, gold ingots, diamond

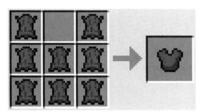

^ Chestplates
Leather, iron ingots, gold ingots, diamond

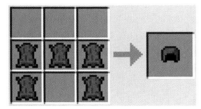

^ Helmets
Leather, iron ingots, gold ingots, diamond

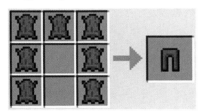

^ Leggings
Leather, iron ingots, gold ingots, diamond

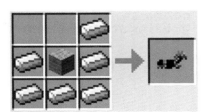

^ Horse armour
Leather, iron ingots, gold ingots, diamond

MECHANISMS

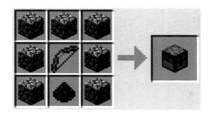

^ Dispenser

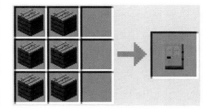

^ Doors
Wooden planks or iron ingots

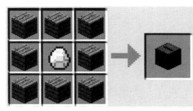

^ Jukebox

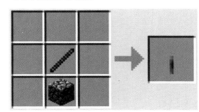

^ Lever

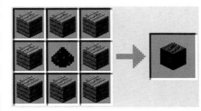

^ Note block

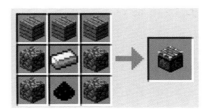

^ Piston

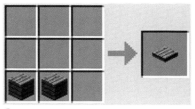

^ Pressure plates
Wooden planks or stone blocks

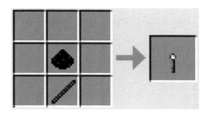

^ Redstone torch

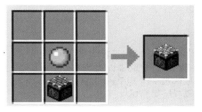

^ Sticky piston

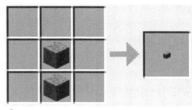

^ Stone button

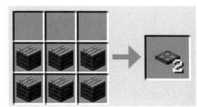

^ Trapdoor

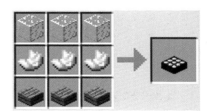

^ Daylight sensor

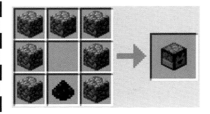

^ Dropper

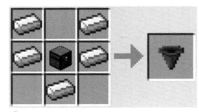

^ Hopper

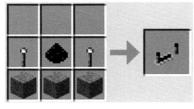

^ Redstone repeater

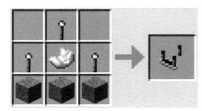

^ Redstone comparator

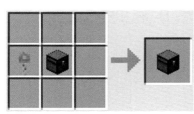

^ Trapped chest

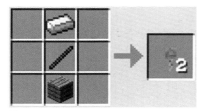

^ Tripwire hook

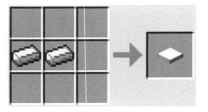

^ Weighted pressure plate
Iron ingots or gold ingots

TRANSPORT

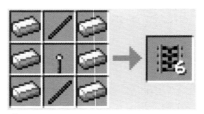

^ Activator rail

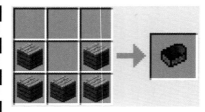

^ Boat

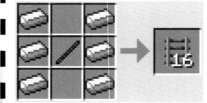

^ Rails

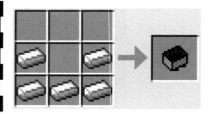

^ Minecart

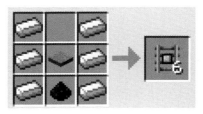

^ Detector rail

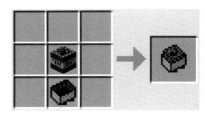

^ Minecart with TNT

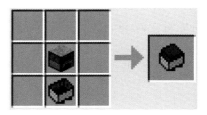

^ Powered minecart

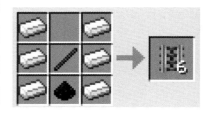

^ Powered rail

ENCHANTMENT

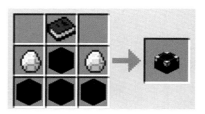

^ Enchantment table

BREWING

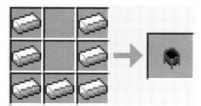

^ Cauldron

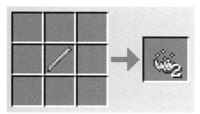

^ Blaze powder

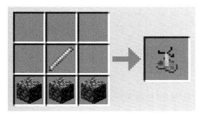

^ Brewing stand

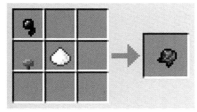

^ Fermented spider eye

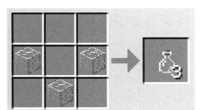

^ Glass bottle

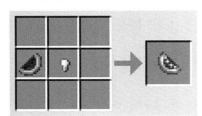

^ Glistering melon

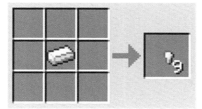

^ Golden nugget

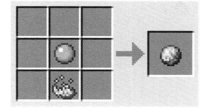

^ Magma cream

WOOL

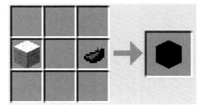

^ Black wool

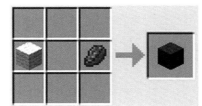

^ Blue wool

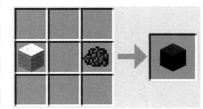

^ Brown wool

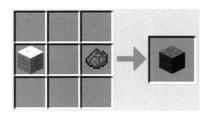

^ Cyan wool

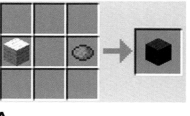

^Gray wool

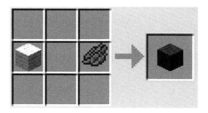

^ Green wool

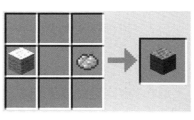

^ Light blue wool

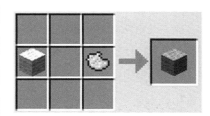

^ Light gray wool

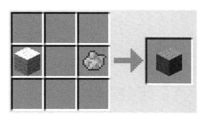

^ Orange wool

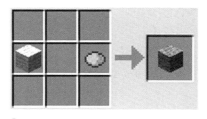

^ Pink wool

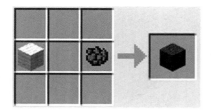

^ Red wool

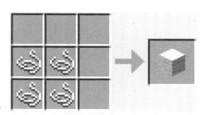

^ Wool block

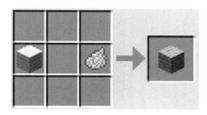

^ Yellow wool

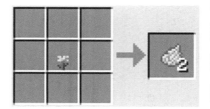

^ Yellow dye

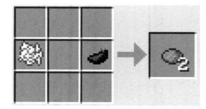

^ Gray dye

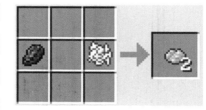

^ Light blue dye

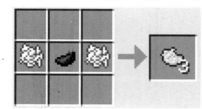

^ Light gray dye

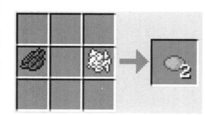

^ Lime dye

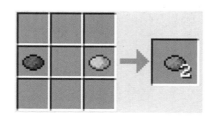

^ Magenta dye

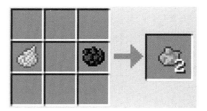

^ Orange dye

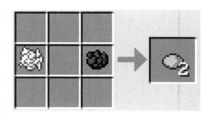

^ Pink dye

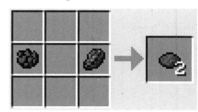

^ Purple dye

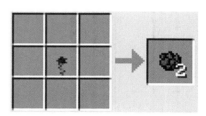

^ Red dye

DYE

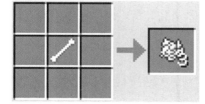

^ White dye

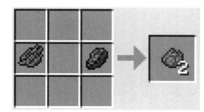

^ Cyan dye

MISC

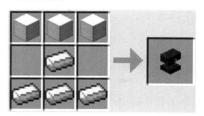

^ Anvil